To my Papa Bear,

Happy 31st Birthday...! It will
certainly be a memorable year!

Finally I get to write in a
book for you. Finally I now
understand the joy it brings...

I love you with all my heart,
Always.

Mama Bear
+ Mini
x X x

25.04.20

Mister Swatch

Mister Swatch

Nicolas Hayek and the Secret of his Success

Jürg Wegelin

Translated by Sophie Leighton

FREE ASSOCIATION BOOKS

First published in Great Britain in 2010 by
FREE ASSOCIATION BOOKS
One Angel Cottages, Milespit Hill, London NW7 1RD

A CIP record for this book is available from the British Library

ISBN 978–1–85343–208–8 hbk

This book is made from paper suitable for recycling and made from fully managed
and sustained forest sources. Logging, pulping and manufacturing processes are
expected to conform to the environmental standards of the country of origin.

10 9 8 7 6 5 4 3 2 1

Produced for Free Association Books by Chase Publishing Services Ltd
Printed and bound in the European Union by
CPI Antony Rowe, Chippenham and Eastbourne

Contents

Preface

Nicolas G. Hayek is a media star. Two articles about him on average appear every day in Swiss newspapers alone. There is hardly any product that is mentioned as often in the editorial pages of the print media as the Swatch. Hayek says that the plastic watch symbolises imagination and enjoyment of life. Yet it also represents something more: its launch in the early 1980s ushered in the resurrection of the Swiss watch industry that was then in deep crisis. Hayek was quick to recognise the underlying potential of this groundbreaking new form of watch. In his report commissioned by the banks, he also established that with its world-famous Omega brand the entire Swiss watch industry was a slumbering leviathan.

The management consultant showed courage. He grasped the opportunity with both hands and invested some of his own capital in the Swiss watch industry, specifically in the ASUAG/SSIH group (Allgemeine Schweizerische Uhrenindustrie AG, and Société Suisse de l'Industrie Horlogère AG) that then formed the core of the sector. This made Hayek the saviour of the Swiss watch. He simultaneously demonstrated with this commitment that mass products could also easily be produced in high-cost Switzerland. Moreover, as Hayek kept preaching, not only the watch industry but Switzerland's entire manufacturing base had a promising future. Labour costs, which constantly served as a reason for moving production to low-wage countries, were no obstacle to the continuation of profitable industrial production in Switzerland. On the contrary, this relocation endangered the long-term position. This man's willingness to back up his optimism with his actions drew great public attention.

Certainly many managers and businesspeople today still blame their failure on what are relatively high labour costs in international terms. Nevertheless, it has since been broadly accepted that Hayek's insight is correct. Emerging as an entrepreneur against the pessimists, he became the nation's economic 'pick-me-up'. Since the 2008 financial crisis, Hayek's life work has gained further topical relevance. Unlike the many gamblers in the financial sector, Hayek embodies the visionary entrepreneur who strives not for short-term profit but for stable growth. Hayek is the long-established boss that the ordinary citizen would like to have. He is entirely different from the hustlers and speculators who only watch share prices. Hayek's relevance to the Swiss economy therefore extends far beyond his services to the watch industry.

The fact that Hayek provided the evidence for the accuracy of his hypothesis with the example of the watch industry has a special significance. Along with Swiss Air, the grounded national airline, or the public-service firms Schweizerische Post and Swiss Federal Railways (SBB), this industry had always played an identity-forging role for Switzerland. The watch industry is an important flagship for Switzerland abroad. The sector embodies typically Swiss values such as accuracy, precision and quality. To recognise this, we only have to remember that the watch industry crisis in the 1970s was a traumatic event on a similar scale to the later demise of the Swiss airline. With his financial commitment and his optimism, Hayek made a vital contribution to creating new confidence. He became a shining example for the entire local economy.

Hayek also demonstrated that his message applied not only to the Swiss economy but to European industry as a whole, which is suffering under pressure from Far Eastern competition. The difficulties of the European car manufacturers, particularly in Germany, which had started long before the financial crisis that emerged in 2008, are in his view certainly not the outcome of an almost inevitable development. They are instead the consequence of misguided company policies. Like the Swiss watch industrialists, the American and European car managers have also spent too long deriding the Japanese as imitators and putting their faith in heavy gas-guzzlers. The standards for eco-friendly future technologies were therefore recently set in the Land of the Rising Sun rather than Europe or the USA. This is one reason why the Japanese car industry was less badly hit by the 2008 economic crisis. In this respect, too, Hayek was one step ahead of his European fellow businessmen. He tried to breathe new life into the European car industry with his ecological Swatch-Car in the early 1990s. At that time he failed because of the conservative attitude of the car bosses. With the debate about global warming, his idea of an eco-friendly car has now also gained fresh impetus in Europe.

It was not only his role in saving the Swiss watch industry, believed to be a lost cause, but also in particular his talent for communication that has made Hayek one of the most sought-after interviewees of the last 20 years. Along with the financial media, the pages of the tabloid and popular press also scramble after him. Hayek is the only business leader who gets asked for his autograph by passers-by in the street. He can hardly walk along the Bahnhofstrasse in Zurich without being approached by someone. 'I get asked what the time is, how many watches I'm wearing, get compliments on a television appearance or old ladies wanting to kiss me', Hayek proudly confided a few years ago to the *Tages-Anzeiger* magazine section.

Despite his popularity, though, the public knows very little about Hayek. When he is photographed crossbow-shooting with top model Cindy Crawford, we only see half the picture. When he appears in public, he puts all his actions, his gestures and statements at the service of marketing his watches. There is hardly any other businessman who masters that as well he does. In such appearances he certainly reveals his talent for showmanship, but not very much more. If we want to understand the maverick Hayek, we must talk to people who have worked with him or know him well personally for other reasons and have intense first-hand experience of him.

In the mid 1970s, as a young employee at the Swiss News Agency (SDA), I had my first opportunity to talk to Hayek. He seemed extremely surprised that a journalist was interested in him. His company Hayek Engineering had just received a commission from the Chinese government to restructure the steel industry. Hayek told me how his consultancy firm had gained this contract from the Ministry of Metallurgy in Beijing. He spoke at great length and gave me a detailed explanation of the reasons why Mao's industrial policies had failed. In the period of the 'Great Leap Forward', the Chinese Communist Party had forced almost every village to run its own small steelworks. After Mao died, the Party wanted to close down these miniature steelworks. The plan was to replace the small-scale steelworkers and undertake the construction of a powerful heavy industry. But after the years of confusion during the Cultural Revolution, there was a lack of specialist workers with the appropriate skills. So the Communist Chinese went against their ideological principles and approached Hayek Engineering, although this company had previously only advised the outlawed Western capitalists. There were two critical factors that determined their choice of the Zurich consultancy firm. First, the Chinese government

wanted to award its contract to a firm that was not closely affiliated
with the interests of the superpowers. Second, Switzerland had been
the first country to recognise the People's Republic of China after the
declaration of independence in 1949.

However, Hayek's breakthrough in the Middle Kingdom received
little attention in Switzerland. The consultant was still relatively
unknown here. And the few people who knew the Lebanese immigrant
tended to scorn him as an outsider. Hayek worked at that time mainly
for foreign clients, in particular for German heavy industry. In Germany
he had discovered a gap in the market and made a name for himself.
His successes there went unnoticed in Switzerland.

After this first phone conversation, I had many further opportunities
to talk to Hayek. In autumn 1985 when he took over the majority stake
in SMH with a group of investors, from which today's Swatch Group
later emerged, this contact became increasingly frequent. Hayek liked
to take a stand not only on the watch industry but also on economic
and political problems. He was very soon one of the best-known
entrepreneurs worldwide. Even the German Chancellor Helmut Kohl
and the French President Jacques Chirac turned to him for advice at
that time. The preacher in the wilderness who had once immigrated
destitute into Switzerland became suddenly a living legend in his new
homeland. Today Hayek is not only the leading entrepreneur but the
'high priest of the watch industry' or, as Franco Cologni, on the board
of directors at the Richemont Group that also operates in the luxury
watch sector, once called him, the 'godfather' of the industry.

However, he is definitely not the 'Father of the Swatch', contrary to
the repeated claims. The reverence goes so far today that Hayek is also
given credit that actually belongs to other people. But he has himself
essentially contributed to this myth-making. 'I have reinvented the
Swiss watch industry, I have created the Swatch', he said a few years
ago in an interview with the French newspaper Le Monde. But this is
not the case: the Swatch was created long before Hayek took over the
watch group. A few years before he was in charge there, the watch
was already successfully emerging in several markets. His statement is
correct if it is understood in its secondary sense: Hayek created what
the Swatch became.

Meanwhile the cult that grew up around Hayek in TV shows and the
popular press has taken on some odd characteristics. With his tendency

towards showmanship, he stands out from the 'grey mice' that are to be encountered at the top of many Swiss firms. When Hayek reveals that he likes swimming naked in his swimming pool, that is a feeding frenzy for the tabloid journalists. This kind of soft news is amusing and no one expects it to be verified. But the reader is still far from knowing what kind of person Hayek really is. 'Mister Swatch' can present himself in the many interviews exactly as he pleases. He can dictate the rules and he makes use of this. One critical article in *Facts* was enough in those days to get the weekly magazine, which has since folded, onto the Swatch Group blacklist.

Unless it is for a home-based feature, interviews with Hayek usually take place in his office at his desk, with Hayek sitting on the boss's high-backed armchair, and the journalist opposite him on the visitor's chair. This creates an atmosphere that is almost reminiscent of a conversation with an employee. If the journalist were actually an employee at the Swatch Group, though, it would hardly occur to him in the bare, old-fashioned decor of this boss's office to ask for a pay rise. Hayek's simple office furnishing makes a sharp contrast with his company's business performance. Since he took over the helm in this watch group around 25 years ago, little has changed in this office. He has just added more mementoes and photos, such as the one inscribed by Cindy Crawford. On the desk there are some Mickey Mouse comics, a biography of Napoleon and, of course, files everywhere. The only expensive item is a Salvador Dali sculpture that Marianne Hayek gave her husband on his 70th birthday. This work of art, which features a softly molten watch hanging on a clothes iron, symbolises a product into which Hayek still puts all his energy and creative force today at the age of over 80. Like the Surrealist artist, Hayek also has his eccentricities. Usually he wears two watches on each wrist. His favourite brands, a luxurious Breguet and a prestigious Omega, almost always take their place next to the loud-ticking Swatch.

Aside from the top boss's flamboyant habits, an atmosphere of sobriety prevails at the administrative headquarters of the Swatch Group at Seevorstadt 6 in Biel. Hayek usually just has a snack at midday. That enables him to hold a sandwich in his left hand and the phone in his right and keep his employees on tenterhooks even during the lunch-break. In January 1989, I visited Hayek just after a management meeting in his office. When I entered, the working lunch had just finished and the secretary was just clearing away the remnants of the modest meal of sandwiches and mineral water. Hayek asked his colleagues on the board of directors, Ernst Thomke – then the number two in the SMH Group as Director-General – and the acting Directors-General Felix Müller and Hans-Jürg Schär, to remain seated at the round table. Schär and Müller did everything they could to avoid disturbing Hayek's one-man show during the interview. Thomke, however, amplified almost every answer his boss gave with an uninvited commentary. The conflict that was soon to break out between the two alpha-leaders could in fact already have been anticipated.

Sooner or later matters had to come to a head between these two dominant personalities. It was logical that Hayek as the equity owner of the company would emerge victorious from this duel. The precise reasons for Thomke's departure, however, remain somewhat obscure. Neither is Hayek's entire past exactly transparent. His life story, especially his youth in Lebanon, is unknown even to his closest colleagues. It is one purpose of this biographical portrait to shed some light on Hayek's origins.

In summer 2007, I informed Nicolas Hayek that I was going to write a biography about him. I asked him if I could come and see him for a few conversations. Hayek replied that he did not want to cooperate with the book. He explained his refusal by saying that 'there are still so many new fascinating projects coming up for me that I prefer to look forward than back'. My intention also to interview third parties for the biography clearly displeased him:

> So you want to summarise a life full of events and actions in a book by getting people to speak – other than me – who have talked to me for an hour at most, or have had various conversations with me in a month, a year, even perhaps two or three years? This life, which please note has so far lasted 4,100 weeks, 28,800 days or – even more impressive – almost 700,000 hours ... writing a proper biography is a big undertaking that in my view cannot be done through a few conversations.

I have nevertheless tackled this undertaking. I have talked to people who did not just know Hayek briefly, but in some cases worked with him closely for years. According to Hayek's argument, only the subject's own memories and information would be relevant for a biography. The memory as we know, however, works in a highly selective way. It also tends to repress or screen out life events that are accompanied by negative feelings. Conversely, events and experiences with positive connotations are given especially strong weight.

It was in fact Hayek himself who gave me the idea of writing a book about him a few years ago. I had asked him in passing after one of my last few interviews whether anyone had yet had the idea of writing his biography. 'You write one!', he replied at the time with his roguish smile. He probably meant it as a joke, as I later had to conclude from his refusal. The Swiss watch magnate does not readily wish to reveal his hand. In fact, others before me have already made similar attempts, such as Oswald Sigg, the former Vice-Chancellor and Spokesman of the Swiss Federal Council. He and the journalist Oliver Fahrni also received a refusal from Hayek years ago. The major French publisher Gallimard also once wanted to commission an author for a biography. Hayek refused. So the public today only knows half of Hayek – the side that he presents himself.

For this biography I have interviewed several dozen current and former close colleagues, as well as competitors and politicians who know Hayek well. I met many long-standing acquaintances in the course of my research. Comments are made here by both admirers and critics. The rules of independent journalism forbade me to name these sources, unless the people concerned had no objections to being identified. I asked Nicolas Hayek once again for an interview after I had completed my work, in order to be able to explain certain outstanding questions in more detail with the aid of his information. However, he refused. He explained to me that he was afraid that this might be interpreted as an authorisation of the book's contents.

For the sake of readability, this biography has a partly chronological and partly thematic structure. It begins with an account of Hayek's youth in Lebanon. I have researched this in Hayek's circle, particularly in Beirut. I have tried to discover the reasons that prompted Hayek to emigrate to Switzerland. I reached the conclusion that it is for the same reasons as those that drove him to become self-employed as a watch industrialist. They stem from Hayek's fierce hatred of being directed by others. In Lebanon it was the family that wanted to force him into a straitjacket of traditional norms. Later it was the customers and banks that he felt were restricting his freedom of action. The fact that a family conflict lay behind the decision to emigrate was previously unknown even to his closest colleagues. But in Switzerland people also tried to put obstacles in the immigrant's way at first.

Two further chapters are devoted to Hayek's consultancy firm, Hayek Engineering. To my knowledge nothing has been written till now about the history of its emergence. It was only his success with this consultancy firm that later enabled Hayek to enter the Swiss watch industry. At this time the Swatch was already on the market. Jochem Thieme, then Hayek's closest colleague in the watch industry, relates here for the first time as an independent witness how this innovative watch came into being. It was not Nicolas Hayek but Ernst Thomke who initiated the project. This paternity dispute between Hayek and Thomke is not, however, the only reason for their quarrel. How and why the rift with Thomke developed is told in detail here for the first time.

The following chapters are devoted to how Hayek turned the Swatch Group into the global leader in the watch industry. Of course the adventurous entrepreneur also experienced a few failures. They do not detract in any way, though, from Hayek's importance for the Swiss economy, as is discussed in the concluding chapter. For only someone who does not undertake anything – in Hayek's terms this is not an entrepreneur – makes no mistakes.

1

Severed Roots – Hayek's Childhood and Youth in Lebanon

WHEN NICOLAS HAYEK ARRIVED in Switzerland in 1949, the immigration of people from different cultures had not yet become a political issue in this part of the world. Certainly in the postwar years there was a constantly increasing number of guest workers from Italy, most of whom worked in the construction industry. There were only very few people from non-European countries – even a Sicilian was regarded as semi-exotic in Switzerland. Although the overwhelming majority of these foreigners came from the southern neighbouring country, the hostility to foreigners was as widespread as it is today. So it is hardly surprising that as a Lebanese immigrant Nicolas G. Hayek had a long battle against prejudices. Being only 1.65 metres tall and speaking broken German, the immigrant immediately drew attention everywhere with his striking nose and bushy eyebrows. Many people clearly assumed he was from southern Italy. 'I was treated like a *Tschingg* then', Hayek told the Ringier journalist Frank A. Meyer a few years ago in the TV programme *Vis-à-vis*. '*Tschingg*' was an abusive term for Italian immigrants at the time.

Foreigners who do not feel accepted react in very different ways. There are some who consciously emphasise their origins by differentiating themselves from their host country through their clothing, behaviour and a rejection of linguistic integration. They try in this way to preserve their identity in a form of subculture. Others repress their foreignness and do everything they can to downplay their ancestry. This is the path Hayek chose. He tries to make his origins invisible. He has so far divulged only a few small fragments of his youth.

Jochem Thieme, one of his closest colleagues at the consultancy firm Hayek Engineering from 1975 to 1985, can only remember one occasion on which his former boss talked about his youth. It was at the beginning of the 1970s in São Paulo. When the two of them were walking through the streets of the Brazilian capital, Hayek suddenly

1

saw a kebab stand. Thieme remembers that he nearly 'freaked out' with joy at this discovery. Unlike Brazil, Western Europe did not yet have these snack stands selling lamb seasoned with mint and onions. Since his childhood Hayek had never had the opportunity to eat this speciality that is enjoyed not only in Turkey but also in Lebanon. The sight and the smell of the seasoned meat brought some long-buried feelings to the surface. However, Hayek has retained to this day the spontaneity and emotionality he then showed towards his colleague, which is rather unusual by Swiss standards.

Nevertheless, the boss of the Swatch Group is very reluctant to be reminded of his Lebanese roots. When he is asked about it, he can even react very brusquely. 'I'm no oriental', he replied, visibly annoyed, when the Western Swiss television interviewer wanted to talk about the subject of Hayek's youth a few years ago. And when Viktor Weber, as editor of the financial newspaper *Cash*, since folded, once broached this subject, Hayek abruptly broke off the interview in annoyance. This is a surprising reaction. Actually the immigrant from the Middle East could be extremely proud that despite the many obstacles initially put in his way he has managed to become one of the most successful and internationally famous businessmen in the country.

Hayek's example should give pause for thought to all those right-wing conservative politicians and voters who only ever see immigration as a danger rather than an enrichment. Hayek is no isolated example. Many foreigners before him have made careers here and made an important contribution to Switzerland's economic, social and cultural development. Some internationally known Swiss firms were founded by immigrants. Frank Saurer, Henri Nestlé, Charles Brown and Walter Boveri are just a few examples. The watch industry also owes its existence to immigrants. Huguenots who fled to Switzerland laid the foundations for many well-known watch brands. Hayek has continued this tradition. But he has simultaneously followed a Lebanese tradition. More than 12 million Lebanese live abroad today, which corresponds to around one third of this small country's population. The Mexican Carlos Slim, one of the richest men in the world, is also from Lebanon.

Not all immigrants in Switzerland find it that easy to adjust to its prevailing customs and conventions and proceed to become enormously rich. Admittedly, with his direct manner Hayek often made a bad impression at first. To integrate into his host country, though, he has made far greater efforts than may be expected from a foreigner who has immigrated. He has completely cut himself off from his original homeland, Lebanon, and drawn a line under his past. He has never returned to the land of the cedars. That is rather unusual, as most Lebanese who emigrate feel a strong tie with their native land. Hayek, however, has almost taken on a new identity. It was his goal to be perceived as a native Swiss in his chosen homeland. So at the Swatch Group there is not a single official company biography that contains even basic details about his youth. No one knew why he immigrated to Switzerland at that time. Even at the highest boardroom level, no one knows anything precise about the top boss's past.

So Hayek has since managed to let the grass grow over his youth. The fact that he still makes some mistakes with articles or cases in the German language even now is hardly striking any more in Switzerland as a country of immigration. Even his unusually strong family feeling by Swiss standards is hardly ever connected with his original homeland influenced by clannish attitudes. At every possible opportunity, Hayek demonstrates his zealous patriotism. Hayek's heart – not only his Swatch – beats unmistakably for this country. He relates that he nearly flew into a tantrum when Islamic fundamentalists in Beirut ignorantly burned a Swiss flag instead of a Danish one because of the Mohammed caricatures published in Denmark.

Perhaps one of the characteristics that enables some immigrants to be successful in their new homeland is their remarkable adaptability. Also immigrants are obviously generally less afraid of taking risks, including that of exclusion. Leaving your land of origin and its familiar environment already entails a certain daring. The sociologist Anne Juhasz concludes from the findings of her Swiss National Fund project on immigrants as entrepreneurs that 'immigrants are exceptional people; they are usually less afraid of failure and are used to living with uncertainties'.

Nicolas Hayek is a good example of the plausibility of this hypothesis. He has hardly ever allowed himself to be discouraged by setbacks. When this red-blooded entrepreneur encounters resistance, it seems instead to spur him on. Even when he already had some demonstrable entrepreneurial successes, many Swiss managers still made him feel that he did not belong with them. He simply did not fit the mould of the traditional Swiss business leader. Some of the criticism came from the highest places. Figures such as Guido Richterich, former President of the Swiss Employers Association and top manager at Hoffroche, commented that he never entered the ranks of the major financial bodies, that he put his own opinion forward very strongly and was always quick to jump in and criticise. For a president of the economic umbrella organisation to reprimand one of his members by name publicly is rather unusual. Such accusations have always deeply affected Hayek. He is extremely easily hurt. 'For a few establishment fundamentalists, I am an outsider who was not born in Switzerland. I am a passionate Swiss who would do anything for this country. But I'm not an army colonel, I'm just a civil defence serviceman. I don't belong to the Zurich elite', Hayek complained in 1995 to the financial newspaper *Cash*. But such criticisms have only ever presented a stronger challenge to Hayek. He wanted to show everyone what he could do.

Yet the days are gone when military rank belonged to the achievement record in many Swiss firms and was a decisive influence on a career. Certainly, for some of the older generation, Hayek is considered a 'bright bird of paradise' even today. Many also resent his strong media presence. Hayek's good connection with his long-standing friend Frank A. Meyer was always observed with great suspicion. So, for example, his 80th birthday on 19 February 2008 certainly received a mention in the tabloid newspaper *Blick* that belongs to the Ringier Group. However, the *Neue Zürcher Zeitung* (NZZ) did not breathe a word about the anniversary celebrant – surprisingly, as the cabaret artist César Kaiser's 80th birthday was considered well worth an article by the 'old aunt', which is still considered an authority on the economy. This discrepancy may, however, have more to do with a lack of sympathy than lack of esteem. For Hayek's services to the Swiss watch industry are acknowledged even by the NZZ. Hardly anyone today still disputes that he is an outstanding personality. For Hayek is more than just a successful business leader.

His rise to become the internationally best-known Swiss businessman was by no means a predestined outcome for him. Nicolas Georges Hayek was born on 19 February 1928 in Beirut. The young Nicolas grew up in a very prosperous environment. Both his father Georges Nicolas and his mother Linda, née Tamer, came from affluent families in Bechmezine, a small town in the northern Koura district. Hayek's mother grew up in a prominent family of lawyers. The father studied dentistry before his marriage in the USA at the Jesuit-run Loyola University in Chicago. Hayek says his father was an American. He never mentions his Lebanese origins. In fact, Hayek's father had both US and Lebanese citizenship. In Lebanon both his parents belonged to the Greek orthodox religious community, one of the nine main Christian religious persuasions in this country.

The origin of the Christians is highly contentious in Lebanon. A research team at the Lebanese American University claims recently to have discovered a direct link between the Christian religious communities in Lebanon and the Crusaders. The knights who battled to reconquer the Holy Land from the twelfth to the fourteenth centuries are supposed to have left some genetic traces. So is Nicolas Hayek a descendant of the 'liberators' of the Holy Land? The Swiss watch magnate vehemently rejects any such supposition. He says that a connection with the Crusaders has always been imputed to the Lebanese Christians. In fact the hypothesis served the Muslims in 1860 among other things as a pretext for the bloody persecution of the Christians.

The Christians long occupied an important position of influence in the fragile power-structure of Lebanon, as did the Hayeks who lived there, of which there is an urban, Maronite branch as well as the rural, Greek Orthodox one. Since Hayek left the country, the Christians have lost some influence, though. Hayek is almost as common a name in Lebanon as Müller or Meier in Switzerland. At the American University in Beirut alone there are well over a dozen students and lecturers named Hayek. An entire district of Beirut is also called El Hayek. Although this is a very common name, most Hayeks belong to the upper class. Hayek's father worked as a dental assistant at the American University after his return from the USA before he opened a dental practice in Beirut. In the American University archives, Hayek's father is listed under the name Nikula Georges Haik (Hayik). The unusual spelling is explained by the back-translation of the name from the Arabic. In Arabic, Hayek refers to the weaving profession.

In Beirut, the Hayeks lived in Abdel Wahab Street in Achrafieh, a rather elegant part of the city that contains the best gourmet restaurants today. This peaceful district, which unlike other parts of the city suffered little damage to its historical buildings during the civil war, has a special charm. Like most prosperous Lebanese, Hayek's parents owned a second house in their home province Koura. This region, approximately 80 kilometres north of Beirut, is known for its high-quality olive oil production. The Hayeks also owned some olive farms there. The young Nicolas would be sent by his parents to the family-owned olive groves to supervise the workers at the harvest. He often spent his holidays in Koura.

Hayek's emotional bond with his Lebanese mother seems to have been significantly stronger than his relationship with his father. His francophone-orientated upbringing and education were influenced by his mother's strong role. On the few occasions when Hayek talked about his youth, he almost only ever mentioned his mother. He spoke about her then, though, with great admiration and love. Although Hayek never returned to Lebanon, he still has good relationships with some of his relatives there. The firm that belongs to his cousins Jean and Gaby Tamer, trading in chemicals, medical equipment and other products, also represents Omega and Swatch in Lebanon. Hayek maintains very lively contact with his sister Mona, who is two years older than him. Despite her advanced age she, too, is still full of energy. She writes her brother emails and still drives a car despite the chaotic Beirut street traffic.

As well as Nicolas Hayek, some other family members have achieved fame. Running parallel to Abdel Wahab Street, where Hayek lived, is Charles Malik Street. The Malik who was honoured by this street name was an uncle of Hayek's. Malik was a highly respected figure not only in the family but the whole country. The Harvard graduate represented Lebanon in various roles at the UN. The lawyer authored key parts of the UN Charter and the Universal Declaration on Human Rights. He played an active role in the social life of Beirut. He took the young Nicolas to cocktail parties with him. Hayek relates that he always had to wear a tie and listen to the often empty small talk of high society.

He does not have a fond memory of these receptions. He still detests excessively formal occasions. He once apologised, saying that ties 'cut off my nerve paths and windpipe. That's why I wear my tie loose.' Even today Hayek still greatly dislikes wearing a tie. That does not prevent him feeling in his element in the worldly atmosphere of the Basel watch trade fair. When Hayek turns up at the million-franc exhibition pavilion, he always encounters far more respect with his throat-restricting tie than the Federal Councillor who pays his respects at this massive annual event. When he moved from being a consultant to a watch entrepreneur, Hayek reached a good Swiss compromise in sartorial matters with an open shirt over the knot of his tie. For until the beginning of the 1980s, he ignored the tie-wearing convention that was then followed in almost all industries.

Hayek's outfit used to be much more unconventional for a Swiss businessman. Until the mid-1980s he went round in Bohemian style with a corduroy jacket and a colourful small scarf tied around his neck in Wild West fashion. He had a pipe wedged between his teeth and a leather pouch full of tobacco always hanging from his hand. Hayek did not yet wear a beard. With his get-up, though, he would have looked more at home in a discussion group in the literary days of Solothurn than at a cocktail party. In business circles, he immediately made a striking impression everywhere. 'This unconventional disposition, together with his origin and his physical size, prejudiced many conventionally-minded and tradition-conscious business leaders against him', says a former politician who knows Hayek very well. Today, even the most conservative Swiss see beyond such external features. In public Hayek quite often appears in an open shirt that reveals his white chest hairs spreading over the two gold chains in his open collar. No one would think of turning up his nose at this any more.

But even as a child Nicolas Hayek seems to have been a non-conformist with unusual self-confidence. When the teacher once asked him to address his fellow pupils and their parents, he trumpeted proudly into the microphone: 'I am called Nicolas the Great and I am a lion.' Hayek was clearly not lost for words even in those days. His parents later told him that he had been a very attractive child and won everyone over with his charm. While almost all mothers say that about their children, Hayek still seems to feel newly flattered every time he relays this compliment. The fact that he repeatedly mentions this anecdote in interviews demonstrates one of his most prominent characteristics: Hayek craves recognition and affection. Unlike most of his colleagues in the boardroom corridors, he makes no secret of his wish to be liked. He admits it. Despite his rather macho traits, Hayek finds it very easy to talk about his feelings and show his emotions. In that respect, he has remained entirely Lebanese.

Hayek's education is typical for a child from the Lebanese upper classes, which are highly cosmopolitan but also extremely religious-minded. At the Jesuit school, the young Hayek received instruction in the catechism every morning. Something that one of the priests told the pupils was that it was forbidden to marry a close relative. This instruction was not so absurd. Like many rural areas of the world, in Lebanon even today marriages occasionally take place between cousins. The priest failed, however, to give a more thorough justification for this taboo. Also he had clearly not reckoned with the young Nicolas who as a maverick was already used to questioning everything all the time. For the attentive pupil immediately remembered the story of Adam and Eve, which the same teacher had told a week before. How, then, Nicolas wanted to know, did Adam and Eve have their children after they were expelled from the Garden of Eden? The priest lost his composure at this impertinent astuteness, went red and found no other solution than to reprimand the pupil.

Such experiences from his conservative religious education may be one reason why Hayek takes a highly ambivalent attitude to religion today. He no longer belongs to any religious community. It may be the same for him as for other prominent figures who cannot be instantly classified – occasionally they especially stimulate the imagination of their fellow citizens. So, for example, Luigi Colani, regarded by the media at the time as a star designer, plied Hayek with offensive anti-Semitic remarks in the mid-1990s. He thereby suggested that he was Jewish. Hayek immediately had this rectified by his press office: 'Mr Hayek is a Christian on his father's side and his mother's side, as well as all his previous ancestors back to Adam and Eve and not – as stated – a Jew.' The fact that Hayek begins Christianity with Adam and Eve shows that he is not one of the most biblically well-versed of Christians. Instead of lambasting the anti-Semitism, it was certainly his intention to correct his religious origin. Although he calls himself a believer today, he has little use for the Church as an institution, as with institutions in general. Rituals, whether religious or secular, are repugnant to him, mainly because they often lack credibility. Also Hayek finds it hypocritical that George W. Bush is deeply religious and a keen churchgoer but that this did not prevent him from waging a war on Iraq that contravened international law with total conviction.

Religious affiliation is an important part of everyone's identity in Lebanon, regardless of whether the person concerned practises the belief. The solidarity with the family and the religious community is much stronger than that with the state. The close integration into the group social network, which extends into professional life, is one reason why the country is so fragmented. 'As a member of a western-orientated Christian minority, I had hardly any contact with the other ethnic groups, least of all Muslims', Hayek once said. The various religious communities in Beirut also live in different districts today: the Christians in the East, in the Gemmayzeh and Achrafieh districts, the Sunnis in the West, in Hamra, and the Shiites and the Palestinian refugees in the South, near the airport. While the church bells ring on a Sunday in the East, in the West and the South the muezzin's call to prayer sounds from the minaret. Most children attend religious schools. The American University of Lebanon is one of the few educational institutions in which young people from the various groups in the population meet. However, Nicolas Hayek completed most of his studies in mathematics, chemistry and physics at the Christian University of Saint-Joseph that was then situated in the district where he lived. The building in which Hayek attended mathematics lectures stands empty today and is derelict. The new building is situated on the other side of the street. This small university already had a partnership then with the University of Lyon, where Hayek studied for one year. When he was 21 years old, he obtained the Certificat de licence, an intermediate diploma, with the 'Mention assez bien', which roughly corresponds to a grade between 'satisfactory' and 'good'.

Although Hayek grew up in an environment that was separate from the Muslim world, he has repeatedly criticised the anti-Islamic attitude that is currently spreading. The Islamic world is also full of peace-loving and warm-hearted people. Fanatics exist not only among Muslims but also increasingly also in Christian circles in Europe and the USA. Hayek states that he would never allow a narrow-minded headscarf debate at the Swatch Group.

The headscarf was never a subject of debate in his former homeland. Despite the boost received there by both Christian and Muslim funda-mentalists since the Civil War, Lebanon today remains one of the most liberal countries in the Arab world. However, this country was never a 'Switzerland of the Middle East', as the Levant state is often called. Apart from the large number of banks, Lebanon and Switzerland have little in common. Even in Hayek's time, great tensions prevailed there between the different groups in the population, for the country had always been at the mercy of foreign interests. After the defeat of the

The Saint-Joseph University building, now derelict, in which Nicolas Hayek attended mathematics lectures.

Central Powers, the Entente occupied the region in 1918. After the First World War, France played an important role in building the young nation. The French received this mandate from the League of Nations and they were supported by the Christian Nationalists. From 1929 to 1931, shortly after Hayek was born, Charles de Gaulle was stationed in Beirut. In contrast, the Arab Nationalists demanded an independent Arab state that would extend far across Lebanon. Yet contrary to the original promises of the League of Nations, Lebanon was not granted independence after the Second World War. In 1943, a Christian–Sunni coalition finally achieved the right to self-determination. Hayek lived through these birth pangs of nation-building at close hand. The strong French influence on the country then also explains the francophone orientation of Hayek's education. The conflict situation that dominates the country can partly be explained by the one-sided advancement of the Christians by the French. If Hayek still lived in Lebanon, he would probably hardly be able to avoid taking sides. It is almost impossible to be politically neutral in Lebanon.

In 1964 Hayek gained Swiss citizenship. On the question of the Israeli–Palestinian conflict, however, he shares the attitude of almost all Lebanese. Like the majority of Swiss, he has certainly always been careful to avoid openly taking sides on this highly sensitive subject. Within the family, however, he is used to expressing his political views extremely forthrightly. There he has always fiercely criticised the Israeli exclusion and attrition policies towards the Palestinians. 'My father had just arrived from Lebanon, a proper Arab, and I remember 1967, the Six Day War in the Middle East, when of course I was the only one at school who did not support Israel', his son Nick once revealed to the magazine section of the *Tages-Anzeiger*.

With hindsight, Hayek regrets that he grew up in an isolated environment and had almost no contact with Muslims in his childhood. Nevertheless, this omission has never led him to get to know his former homeland a bit better subsequently. The information bulletin from the International College (in Hayek's time this school was called the AUB Preparatory School), where he took his final school exams in 1947, once asked in an interview with the former pupil what he still remembered about his youth. 'I remember the beach in Beirut and Beit Mery, with its wonderful view of the Mediterranean Sea. I regret no longer being able to speak the language. I can't find the words any more.' That was it! It is as if Hayek had pressed the delete button at this point in his brain, which still functions like a supercomputer today. The otherwise very cosmopolitan-minded businessman not only keeps his distance from his native land; he has erased or at least shut out his memories.

Nonetheless, Hayek does not seem to be letting go of his youth completely. His sister Mona had to promise to send him all the photos from his childhood. She says that just before his 80th birthday she sent him the last pictures she could find. It seems almost as if Hayek wants to shut this chapter of his life along with the pictures into a box. All the same, he cannot, of course, avoid being repeatedly reminded of his origins. In Beirut it is said that the former Prime Minister Rafic Hariri, who was later assassinated, had asked rich Lebanese abroad at the time to contribute to the reconstruction of the war-torn country. Hayek is said to have refused. Nevertheless, the Lebanese are very proud of their famous son, who made a career abroad. When, at the beginning of the 1990s, the drugs policy created a great stir because of the open drugs scene at the abandoned Letten station in Zurich, people in Switzerland liked to talk about the 'Lebanese drugs mafia'. The generalisation seemed to fan new prejudices and the Lebanese ambassador realised that his country's reputation was under threat. He reminded the local press that many outstanding figures in society, such as Nicolas Hayek, were in fact of Lebanese origin.

A few years ago the National Heritage Foundation in Lebanon organised an exhibition about 16 prominent sons and daughters of the country. As well as such famous figures as the Renault Group boss Carlos Ghosn, Nicolas Hayek was naturally among them. Then the American University in Beirut wanted to award Hayek an honorary doctorate. Yet even this distinction could not entice him to Lebanon. According to his sister, he stayed away because of the assassination of the former Lebanese premier, Hariri. Of course, she was very disappointed that her brother did not come to Beirut. She had already bought a dress for the ceremony. Hayek gives a slightly different explanation for staying away: 'I would have had to take part in a whole load of social functions there. And I hate that.' The explanation does not sound very plausible. When the University of Bologna awarded Hayek an honorary doctorate in 1998, he completed a real assault course of ceremonial occasions. For this opportunity he even had a string of journalists flown into the northern Italian city to publicise the honour more widely. For Hayek this ceremony was actually a highlight of his life. In the laudatory speech he was described as one of the ten most important entrepreneurs of the late twentieth century and mentioned in the same breath as the Microsoft founder, Bill Gates. Hayek took his place alongside a host of celebrities such as the former French President François Mitterrand, the Spanish King Juan Carlos, Nelson Mandela and Mother Teresa. He was now Doctor *honoris causa* of the oldest university on the European continent. Hayek later received many further distinctions, such as an honorary doctorate from the University of Neuenburg in 1996. The French government appointed him an Officer of the French Legion of Honour. In 2007 Hayek was awarded the Lifetime Award on Swiss television. He received this honour not only for his entrepreneurial activities but for his life's work. One million television viewers followed the prize-giving ceremony, at which the former Federal Councillor Adolf Ogi gave the laudatory speech. Hayek was visibly moved, for this honour came as something completely unexpected. Although he had been a Swiss citizen for over 40 years, this selection by the television audience meant something like a form of knighthood for the immigrant.

Nicolas Hayek receiving the Lifetime Award in 2007. On the right, former Federal Councillor Adolf Ogi, who gave the laudatory speech. © SF/Heinz Stucki. 'Swiss Award – the Millionen-Gala 2006', Swiss television, 13.1.2007.

Hayek feels not only Swiss but also European. The cultural and linguistic European influence on his education plays a decisive role here. His sister Mona lived in Paris for a long time and speaks perfect French. His brother Sam, three years younger, studied in Denver, Colorado, and chose an entrepreneurial career path like Nicolas. The two brothers look alike. In his career, though, Sam had distinctly less success. Unlike his brother, he experienced considerable difficulty recovering from setbacks.

Hayek's youth in Lebanon has certainly had a much stronger influence on him than he likes to admit publicly today. The Lebanese have been a trading people since Phoenician times, for around 3,000 years. Hayek is, of course, much more than a trader; he is a brilliant salesman, but he did not acquire this ability at any school. Instead, it seems to run in his veins. 'With his persuasive powers, he could sell an Eskimo a fridge', says a former colleague at Hayek Engineering. Nevertheless, when he was young his interests lay more in the hard sciences than in commercial matters.

With his diploma in mathematics, chemistry and physics only just in his pocket, Hayek moved to Switzerland. There was a very specific reason for his choice of Switzerland as a new homeland. When he was still in Lebanon he had fallen in love with the Swiss Marianne Mezger, two years his junior, who was working as an au pair in a Lebanese family. She was doing what around 100,000 girls from Sri Lanka, the Philippines and Africa do today in prosperous Lebanese households. So she had very low social status according to the notions there. Hayek's parents were opposed to a marriage. They regarded the liaison as unbefitting to their social rank. This way of thinking is still very widespread today in the country, and at that time the codes were very much stricter. It was the custom at that time for the young man wanting to marry to present the girl of his choice to his parents first. Then, if they were in agreement with the connection, the parents would ask for the hand of the chosen person. Nicolas Hayek did not want to bow to this old-fashioned custom. He ignored his parents' wishes. The family conflict that arose from this explains not only his decision to emigrate to Switzerland but also the ambivalent relationship that Hayek still has with his past in Lebanon.

Hayek did not have an easy start in the new homeland. He came to Switzerland with almost no means. He first completed a work placement in the mathematical division at Schweizer Rückversicherung (today SwissRe). It was a job that wasted many of his abilities. In 1951 he married Marianne Mezger without his parents' blessing. In the same year their daughter Nayla was born and, three years later, Georges Nicolas, known as Nick. Hayek says that he did not originally plan to come to Switzerland at all. He had wanted to study nuclear physics in the USA. But he was glad that he had changed his plans. 'After the war, I was convinced that nuclear physics would be used in the service of peace in future. That later turned out to be the wrong conclusion though. If I had chosen nuclear physics as a career path I would have felt today that I had failed in life.' However, Hayek never studied at the Swiss Federal Institute of Technology (ETH) in Zurich. This incorrect report has been copied by various journalists from each other over the years. When I tried to investigate the background at ETH, the Swatch Group issued a press release to clarify this.

The Ed. Mezger engineering works and iron foundry in Kallnach in the Bern canton, where Nicolas Hayek gained his first business experience at his father-in-law's firm in 1952.

By chance the young immigrant's career took a totally unexpected turn. Hayek's father-in-law was suddenly taken into hospital because of a stroke. His firm, the Ed. Mezger engineering works and iron foundry in Kallnach in the Bern canton, was left without a boss. Eduard Mezger's sons were not in a position to stand in for their father at that time. One was only just 15 years old, and the other had pursued a completely different career as a violinist. 'My wife and my mother-in-law implored me to take over the management of the company', Hayek remembers. So despite his basic knowledge of German he jumped in at the deep end without any professional experience. He had not the least idea about the brake pads and moulding machines that this company produced.

But that was not his only handicap. Hayek had enormous difficulty gaining acceptance from the staff at first because of his poor knowledge of German. The farming environment that he entered there in Seeland in the Bern canton was deeply conservative. The foundry and engineering works is situated in the middle of Ackerland. The company still exists today in the industrial estate at Kallnach. The old brick building with the tall chimney is a reminder of early industrialisation, and in front of the building next to the industrial sidings are mountains of cast iron waste. Hayek first had to gain a position in this alien environment. He soon managed, however, to establish the necessary authority. He also sometimes worked with his own hands in the workshop and sought out direct contact with the staff. After a few months he could at least master enough Swiss German to show his 20 colleagues clearly how things should be done.

Although still speaking only broken German, in 1956 Hayek travelled alone to the International Iron Foundry trade fair in Düsseldorf and set up a small stand single-handed. With great dedication he extolled to visitors the sand-machines used in the foundries that were manufactured by the firm Mezger. As he was not yet familiar with the rules and functioning of this specialist trade fair, he obtained the necessary information from his fellow exhibitors with targeted questions. He soon also managed to engage a woman to look after the stand for him who distributed the publicity material and his business card to visitors. Meanwhile, Hayek bustled around at the exhibition and eagerly did some networking, as a visitor to the trade fair at the time remembers.

As a budding entrepreneur, Hayek could very soon demonstrate his first successes. He managed, for example, to obtain a large contract from the Swiss Federal Railways for the supply of brake pads. That enabled the Mezger company to buy the factory space that had so far been rented. This gained the company greater independence.

In time Hayek's father-in-law, Eduard Mezger, recovered from his stroke. After a brief convalescence, he was able to return to the company and take up the reins again. Then the sparks began to fly, not only in the foundry furnaces but also in the interpersonal relationships. During his father-in-law's absence, Hayek had in fact got used to being the boss. He could have his way as he pleased and did not have to answer to anyone. Now that his father-in-law was back in charge he experienced some difficulty in submitting to the company owner. Today Hayek tries to play down the quarrel at that time. 'When two top tenors sing in an orchestra, it cannot work', he says. Yet the conflict has left much deeper traces than this statement might suggest. Hayek's relationship with his wife Marianne's family is still very tense today, as his brother-in-law Fritz Mezger confirms. However, he does not want to comment on the conflicts at that time.

Hayek undoubtedly felt constrained in this patriarchally run family business. He made many suggestions then that were never taken up. 'I was always told, "We tried that once before. You'd do better to focus on your own work."' It is not Hayek's style just to sit out conflicts. Just after the company boss's return he therefore drew his own conclusions and left the firm. He wanted to stand on his own two feet at last. He had learnt a great deal in the Mezger firm, gathered some valuable experiences and got to know a large number of people in the foundry and engineering sector.

Hayek had met Lester B. Knight, founder of the consultancy firm Knight Wendling, at an exhibition in the USA. Knight suggested that he set up a subsidiary in Switzerland. Hayek agreed. As he had no money, he had to pay for his stake with a bank loan. Hayek rented an office at Bahnhofstrasse 11 in Zurich from an energy company as a sub-lessee.

At first Hayek took a room in a guest house. His wife and the two children stayed behind in Aarberg, in the Bern canton. Only later did the whole family move to Schinznach Bad in the Aargau canton. At this stage Hayek seems to have determined to settle in Switzerland, despite the attitudes he encountered as a foreign immigrant, and he had ruled out ever returning to Lebanon.

Professionally, Hayek also had to fall out of favour. He had a difficult start as a consultant. Hayek relates that on the first day of work, 1 August 1957, he had been very depressed. As the first August fireworks were being lit outside, he had sat in the office with tears in his eyes. Since he did not even have his own phone in his office, he had to go and make calls from the booth in the post room opposite. The contracts he had hoped for did not materialise. He received one refusal after another. Two potential customers he knew from his time at the foundry in Kallnach left him hanging, despite their original promises. 'One of these former customers told me his boss felt I was still too young for a consultancy contract.' Hayek did not give up hope, though. He was convinced that sooner or later he would be able to turn the contacts he had made at Mezger to good account.

After a while he suddenly made a breakthrough. He carried out his first contract for the fee of 10,000 German marks for a parts foundry. Now he had finally created a springboard from which he could set about expanding his contacts in the neighbouring northern country. Germany was still engaged in repairing the severe devastation of the Second World War. Industrial reconstruction was well under way. The billions in aid that the USA was providing to war-torn Europe through the Marshall plan had made these markets a real gold mine for resourceful entrepreneurs. Hayek knew how to exploit this. He gradually managed to make a name for himself in the northern adjacent country. Soon he had a clientele that included companies such as the Mannesmann Group.

Now the moment had come for Hayek finally to become self-employed. For some time he had no longer been getting on especially well with his partner, Knight. Also, Hayek had earned some money in the meantime. In 1962, he could afford to build his own house in Meisterschwanden. The Hayeks chose this place of residence in Aargau by pure chance. When his son Nick went on a school trip to Lake Hallwil with his class, Marianne Hayek accompanied the first-formers to give the teacher some support in supervising the children. They then passed this beautifully situated plot of land on which the Hayeks still live now. The villagers are very proud today of their prominent residents. The 2,100-strong community has always taken a very good view of Hayek for not moving to a more favourable tax environment, as the former UBS President, Marcel Ospel, or the head of Novartis, Daniel Vasella, have done. So Meisterschwanden made the multibillionaire and his wife Marianne Citizens of Honour in 2008. Thanks to Hayek, Meisterschwanden is the municipality with the second-lowest taxes today in the Aargau canton. Schinznach Bad may certainly since have regretted not gaining Hayek as a citizen at that time. The taxation level now, for lack of heavy tax-payers, is one third higher there than in Meisterschwanden.

Hayek is an extremely thrifty person. Yet the quality of life that he enjoys at Lake Hallwil is obviously more important to him than the millions that he has to hand over to the treasury in the village. Hayek once said that it would be a nightmare for him to have to live in the tax haven of Monaco. The rich and the super-rich are certainly an important clientele for him. But he seems to feel much happier among ordinary citizens. Among them he also enjoys the greatest admiration. 'I have always sensed Mr Hayek's bond with his homeland community, without his having had to express this by getting involved in village politics', wrote the Meisterschwanden resident Hans Ulrich Fischer, entrepreneur and former Free Democratic Party (FDP) cantonal parliament member, on the occasion of Hayek's 80th birthday. Nicolas Hayek certainly joined the Lake Hallwil tennis club when he had just arrived in Meisterschwanden. Yet Hayek is an individualist rather than a joiner of clubs. The villagers no longer get to see their two Citizens of Honour all that often. However, many still remember how Hayek once helped to assemble beds in the civil defence or how he always went to cast his vote in the urn at the voting office on Sundays in his track suit.

For Hayek there are two important things in his life: his family and his company. Even people who had many dealings with him have never got really close to him. Hayek is certainly extrovert and does not shrink from showing his feelings. Yet apart from his family members, there is hardly anyone to whom he has really opened up. His family, in particular his wife Marianne, are among the few people in whom he has complete trust and on whom he is convinced he can totally rely. Hayek repeatedly emphasises how important a supporting role his wife has provided. 'Without her I would have got no further than being a stationmaster', he once said. This certainly understates the case. However, it is one of the very rare understatements made by Hayek. Generally he prefers – especially where his watches are concerned – to use the superlative.

2

A Sharp Eye and Strong Gut Instincts – Forming Hayek Engineering

THERE WAS NEVER ANY real danger of Nicolas Hayek ending his career as a stationmaster. In his wife Marianne he had someone who was a beacon of calm at home who did not interfere with him. That enabled him to concentrate entirely on his professional career. However, there are other reasons for the entrepreneurial success that then began. Hayek has abilities that are rarely found in this combination. Even his worst enemies have to admit that his strengths far exceed the normal measure. Talents of this kind often have a much stronger influence on an entrepreneurial career than a bag full of schoolbooks.

Jochem Thieme, who worked for Hayek for around 15 years and was able to observe him extremely closely, describes him as follows: 'Never before or since have I met anyone with that kind of combination of qualities: high intelligence, a memory like an elephant, the ability to think extremely fast, diligence and endless energy, coupled with an almost feminine intuition.' These capacities cannot be acquired even at the most famous university.

'He has a kind of sixth sense', according to another long-term colleague at Hayek Engineering. Hayek generally makes decisions by following his feelings or, in the conventional expression, his gut instinct. He usually picks up on developments and trends long before anyone else. To give one small example: although Hayek himself never used a computer then, he recognised the significance of electronics for the everyday lives of consumers even in the early 1980s.

However, a company cannot be run by intuition alone. Hayek also has strong analytical skills and the capacity for strategic thinking. Hayek can immediately distil the most important elements from a confusing jumble of figures and draw the necessary conclusions. He can break down complicated connections into the essentials. Once Hayek has formed an opinion, it is usually very difficult to dissuade him. Thieme says in retrospect that he almost always had to acknowledge that Hayek was right. Not everyone reacts to this in the same way. For some people this ostentatious self-assurance creates the confidence that Hayek is certainly right. Others find this self-confidence arrogant. Hayek tends to polarise people around him. 'Anyone who gets to know him respects him and even maybe adores him or alternatively hates him. We owed 90 per cent of our contract portfolio entirely to him. On the other hand, in 90 per cent of the contracts that we lost, he was the reason why the client took off', says a former consultant at Hayek Engineering.

His sharp eye for new trends and developments may have reinforced Hayek's autocratic leadership style. Why follow other people when in the end you are usually right yourself? In meetings Hayek is often the only person who still knows after two hours of discussion which of the two dozen participants said what when. So he can immediately and relentlessly find contradictions in the arguments made by his discussion partners and so impose his own viewpoint. Even at the age of over 80, Hayek can still make his much younger colleagues look old with his phenomenal memory.

Hayek laid the foundation stone for his professional success at the age of 35 when he set up Hayek Engineering. This consultancy firm only really made the headlines though when Hayek became involved in the watch industry. Apart from this contract, which Hayek publicised, very little is known even today about this firm's activities. It was also never company policy to put information about the course of business or customers into the public domain.

It is the period up to 1985 – before Hayek took a financial stake in the ASUAG/SSIH group – that is of foremost interest here, for from 1988 Hayek was mainly focusing on the watch industry. Since becoming a watch entrepreneur, he has just kept his involvement in the Zurich consultancy firm ticking over. The company did not make the headlines again until 1999, when it carried out a site evaluation for the Swiss National Exhibition at the request of the Expo 02 Strategic Committee and the Federal Council. It is therefore not surprising that firms such as McKinsey or the Boston Consulting Group left Hayek Engineering far behind in the years that followed in the domain of company reor-

ganisations and strategy development. Today Hayek Engineering is no
longer a management consultancy firm in the narrower sense. The firm
concentrates primarily on construction and engineering. For instance,
it took overall control of the project management for the new terminal
expansion of Cologne airport.

Previously Hayek Engineering still participated in complex company
reorganisations and restructurings. At first most of the commissions
came from Germany. Up to the end of the 1960s, Switzerland was a
market of rather secondary importance for the consultancy firm. Even
most of the employees came from the neighbouring northern country.
When he set up his own firm in 1963, Hayek took with him most of
the core workforce of the consultancy firm that he had previously run
with his partner, Lester Knight. Most of his employees were German
professionals who flew or drove to Zurich every Monday and returned
home at the weekend.

Hayek had soon made a name for himself in Germany as a specialist
in the construction and reorganisation of steelworks and foundries.
He knew this sector inside out; after all, he had in fact temporarily run
his father-in-law's foundry in Kallnach in the Bern canton. Through
these contracts, Hayek Engineering flourished from the outset. German
heavy industry in the Ruhr region, largely destroyed in the Second
World War, was entering a rapid development. Hayek identified a gap
in the market there. The consultant who started in 1957 with a few
thousand francs in startup capital and without his own phone turned
into a prosperous management consultant.

Hayek acquired an office building in Zurich city centre. At the
time Uli Prager had just opened his first Mövenpick restaurant on
the ground floor of the austere building. The still highly unusual,
for many people exotic, smells in those days that emerged from the
pioneering gastronome's experimental kitchen spread throughout the
whole building; in the Hayek Engineering offices on the top three floors
there was often an overwhelming smell of curry. But Nicolas Hayek
was not too bothered by that. However, some of his employees found
these emanating smells highly embarrassing when clients came to see
them. The premises in Dreikönigstrasse 21 never provided an especially
stylish ambiance for receiving clients. But the business leaders of the
rust-laden German heavy industry who called there did not seem to
be all that fastidious. Anyway, if necessary Hayek could accommodate

them in the Hotel Baur au Lac nearby with a view over the lake. The Diagonal, the luxury hotel's bar, became the regular venue for the Hayek staff at the end of the working day.

The open-plan offices of Hayek Engineering must have looked distinctly old-fashioned to visitors. Whereas other companies had very early introduced electronics, at Hayek Engineering half a dozen mechanical adding-machines stood on the desks even up to the mid-1980s. When the employees operated the crank at the side, a precursor of the 'enter' button on a PC today, to input the calculating operation, a nerve-jangling noise filled the space. The computer age was late to arrive at Hayek Engineering.

In the early 1980s, concerning the headcount at the consultancy firm, imaginary figures of up to 350 employees were in circulation. Almost no one but Hayek knew the precise headcount. The project managers were directed by him to specify in client negotiations a workforce of a few hundred people. Former employees estimate that the company actually never employed more than 40 people. To these salaried employees though were added a whole series of freelancers who were recruited as necessary for specific contracts. Some employees also worked on short-term contracts.

Acquiring contracts was always the boss's business. As a wily networker Hayek landed one contract after another. He had early managed to engage a European expert in the metallurgy field, the ETH Professor Robert Durrer. Durrer worked for Hayek on a contract basis. The scientist had developed a procedure with the firm Roll in Gerlafingen with factory trials in which pure, industrially produced oxygen was blown into the steel crucibles. This invention had revolutionised the steel industry in the industrial countries. Even today half of all steelworks worldwide use this procedure. The German ETH professor also made a vital contribution to filling the order books at the Zurich consultancy firm. Over time, increasing numbers of individual enquiries also came from the Far East, for instance from China and Thailand.

Hayek got on extremely well with Professor Durrer. Otherwise, though, Hayek never had a high opinion of academics. Unlike McKinsey, he did not like to recruit people straight from university. For him, a university diploma was anything but an advantage for an appointment. He most preferred specialists with a proven track record in industry. A consultant who had never borne operational responsibility in production or put any of his ideas into practice was lacking something essential, in Hayek's view. He preferred proficient toolmakers and metalworkers or highly experienced bookkeepers.

He once asked one of his young academic employees why he had such a grey view of the world. 'Doctor Scholl,' Hayek said, with a slightly ironic emphasis on the word 'Doctor', 'you know, the world is not nearly as complicated as you imagine.' Eric Scholl, who had just handed in his dissertation on 'Computer-assisted synthesis planning' at Bern University, soon saw which way the wind was blowing. He had to realise that the theoretical knowledge he had gained at the University had no great status in his new place of work. 'If you send a donkey to music college in Salzburg, you won't turn him into a Mozart, and if you send a camel to do an MBA, you won't turn him into a Henry Ford', Hayek used to repeat in various interviews. He constantly denigrates university qualifications. After all, he is living proof that they are not necessary.

Unlike many other Swiss business leaders, he could not rely on any old-boy network from the army or the Rotary Club. But at a time when the concept of networking still sounded exotic, Hayek eagerly developed contacts with people he thought might be useful to him one day. Through successfully completed contracts from well-known firms such as Krupp, Mercedes, Krauss-Maffei, Kloeckner, AEG and Volkswagen but also for the World Bank in Brazil and the South Korean government, he built up a large, high-calibre relationships network.

In this way he got to know better Toni Schmücker, the former Chairman of Rheinstahl (later Thyssen Stahl) and later at Volkswagen. Hayek also cultivated very good relationships with the Bavarian Christian Democratic Union (CDU) politician Franz Joseph Strauss, Princess Thurn und Taxis and the Federal Chancellor, Helmut Kohl. He was always very proud of these connections. He mentions the names of these high-profile acquaintances at almost every possible opportunity. Hayek loves to confound his conversation partner with this kind of namedropping.

However, these many acquaintances have only rarely led to close friendships. The former Chairman of Dresdner Bank and later German Finance Minister, Hans Friedrichs, was one of the few acquaintances that developed into a very close relationship. Together with Hayek,

Friedrichs brought the middle-class Swabian businessman Heinz Dürr
to the top of AEG. Dürr was to lick the ailing electrical company
back into shape. But his reorganisation attempt failed. Friedrichs has
described how he contrived this appointment together with Hayek in
his commemorative publication, *Heinz Dürr. Approach to a curious
entrepreneur*. Friedrichs said to Dürr:

> Remember. We met Niki Hayek during my home leave in St Moritz ...
> We wanted to inspire you with enthusiasm to take on the task. And Niki
> Hayek said in one of the conversations with me afterwards: 'The key to this
> is probably his wife. She is the person we must convince.' So we included
> your wife in our efforts and we succeeded.

This anecdote illustrates the importance Hayek has always attached to
'soft factors' in business matters. This sensitivity towards them cannot
be acquired on any management course. Many 'big shots' in business
lack it. Hayek did not always find it easy, though, to convince his
clients with such arguments.

Consultants have always had the reputation of being notorious
know-alls. Many of them beat their clients about the ears with grand-
sounding terms like 'value management' and suchlike in an effort to
impress them. Once their suggestions have been implemented, they
no longer have to answer for the consequences of the measures. It
is no wonder that the consultancy sector does not have the best of
reputations everywhere. Unlike his famous competitors such as
McKinsey, Hayek always adopted a highly pragmatic approach. His
motto was: 'We only recommend to our clients what we are willing to
implement ourselves.' Nevertheless, the Hayek people also constantly
had to defend themselves against being criticised as know-alls. Once
when the Hayek team sent from Zurich arrived to start a contract at the
Kloeckner-Hütten factory in Bremen, a sign hung on their office door
on Monday that read, 'Consultants are like eunuchs; they know what
it's about but they can't do it.' The saying had been copied by a few
staff members from an article in *Der Spiegel*. This mockery was water
off a duck's back, though, for Hayek's people. They certainly did not
regard themselves as entrepreneurial castrati, for at Hayek Engineering
a project manager always had to reckon on being assigned by the top
boss to implement his own proposals in practice in accordance with
the presentations. For example, a Hayek consultant might easily be

sent to Nigeria for a year to run a steelworks there and implement the strategy he had recommended.

However, not all the contracts had such an exotic quality. Moreover, the company was slowing gaining a foothold in Switzerland, too. For instance, Hayek sent his younger brother Sam, who worked with him for 14 years, as an 'interim manager' to Sibra, then the biggest Swiss drinks company, in Freiburg. Every morning at seven they had a brainstorming session on the telephone. The plan was to reposition the beer brand Cardinal. The beer cartel that long operated the most restrictive market collusion among Swiss suppliers was breaking up. On his brother Nicolas's advice, Sam tried by increasing production capacities and drastically cutting prices to exploit the breakup of the market organisation to his advantage. This headlong endeavour foundered, though. The expansion with alcohol-free beer abroad also ended in failure. The bottling plant project for Moussy beer in the Arab region had to be abandoned at the last minute. Sibra suddenly went into the red because the brewery had established overcapacities. The Cardinal brand was swallowed up by Feldschlösschen. Sam Hayek often used to jest in personal conversation that he did not know much about beer. The course of events seemed to prove him right. Nevertheless, this flop did not do too much damage to Hayek Engineering, for only very few people knew that not Sam Hayek but his brother's consultancy firm was ultimately responsible for this contract.

Yet Hayek Engineering was generally successful in its reorganisation proposals. When the consultancy firm had to muster the evidence for the accuracy of its recommendations, of course it took some risks, as in the case of Sibra. This was in total contrast to McKinsey: in the overhead value analysis it had developed, with its cost-cutting focus, this firm was selling a product. The risk was then always borne entirely by the client. The drastic remedies recommended by McKinsey, targeted at reducing costs, were usually connected with redundancies. The long-term consequences of such stringent reduction measures are difficult to assess in advance. If negative developments later ensue, the consultants can no longer be called to account.

By contrast, Hayek Engineering never went to clients with a ready-made formula. The consultants always tried to take soundings on the ground first. Before analysing the figures, they first carefully investigated soft factors, such as the working atmosphere, the informal structures and procedures, and so on. The Hayek people held conversations with everyone down to the least skilled worker and only then undertook an analysis of the problem. Here, too, though, the main objective was usually to lower costs. 'Production costs are not God-given', Hayek would preach to his people. For him, though, getting a grip on costs did not always require redundancies. Optimising procedures and improving the production process or the stockkeeping can often generate much bigger savings.

However, the pragmatism that prevailed at Hayek Engineering went a bit too far for some employees. Once a fellow executive suggested to Hayek that employees who were not taking part in a project at any given time should be assigned to evaluating reports that had been prepared in the past. Yet this idea did not find favour with Hayek and he let the suggestion hang in the air. No attempt was ever made to draw any systematic lessons from the results of all the operational analyses undertaken. No practical guidelines were ever derived for later, similarly structured contracts. There was also no formalised process for knowledge transfer inside the company.

Hayek was the only pivotal point through which knowledge was transferred. For he took an active part in all the projects. He sometimes added caustic comments in the margin like 'Blah, blah, blah' or 'Oh dear' to the report drafts written by employees. Hours of discussion then followed Hayek's criticisms. No report could leave the building unless it had been signed off by the top boss. The final version of the imitation leather-bound studies inscribed with gold lettering was always personally signed by Hayek. He did not like his people gaining too high a profile outside the company. Former employees suspect that he was afraid that his consultants might try to raise their market value, which would bring the danger of their being poached by the competition. One or other of them might have had the idea of setting up independently. After all, this is what Hayek had done himself when he broke away from Knight.

Hayek likes to keep as much as possible under his control. He would keep his employees on their toes with phone calls not only from his home but also from his holidays in Cap d'Antibes in the South of France or the long weekends skiing in St Moritz. He always wanted to be kept up-to-date with everything. No sooner had he arrived at the piste in the morning with the Corviglia train than he was on the

Nicolas Hayek, 1975. © Keystone.

phone, and once he had skied down the slope he would ring someone
up again. At the relatively small consultancy firm it was still much
easier for him then to get an overview than today at the large Swatch
Group. Nevertheless, Hayek Engineering reached a size at the end
of the 1970s that made it increasingly difficult for him to control
absolutely everything. Several overseas branches were opened. The
company was no longer so one-sidedly focused on Germany, as at
the beginning. The US branch in New Jersey, for example, managed
to land some interesting contracts in the 80,000-ton foundry of John
Deere, the world-famous producer of agricultural machinery and the
International Harvester. Offices were also opened in Britain and Brazil.
Hayek Consultores Ltd in São Paulo gained a massive contract from
Aços Villares with a feasibility study and the development of a master
plan for a new stainless steelworks. The World Bank provided $300
million for the project.

  For this huge contract Hayek Consultores would have had to
quintuple its headcount of 20 employees, but Hayek blew the deal
at the last minute because of a quarrel about paying for a few airline
tickets. In the Hayek Engineering offices, his employees shook their

heads in disbelief. Of course, the paltry sum that this airline ticket represented in relation to the fee in prospect could hardly be the real reason for pulling out. Hayek's employees suspected instead that their boss was afraid that this Latin American outpost would gain such great importance that it could develop an independent existence far away from the control of the Zurich head office. A foreign branch of a consultancy firm that acquires its own contracts has in fact much more independence than the daughter company of an industrial firm such as the Swatch Group today. Their capital is their personal connections in the relevant country rather than the finances of the Swiss headquarters. In any case, Hayek sacked the entire workforce of the newly established branch in São Paulo overnight and closed down the firm.

The resourceful entrepreneur whose strength it had always been to keep sensing new opportunities to develop his business had evidently blocked a highly promising possibility for expansion in South America. Hayek does not find it easy to trust people, according to former employees. In his consultancy firm, a real corporate spirit could therefore never develop in the way achieved by his competitors with partnership and participation models.

Like most companies, at Hayek Engineering there were certainly also the usual staff occasions to cultivate a good working atmosphere. So the traditional Christmas party usually took place at the Carlton Hotel or at the Mövenpick Beef Club on the ground floor of the Hayek building. The mood could sometimes be truly relaxed and enjoyable. An extremely special occasion took place on the 15th anniversary of Hayek Engineering that was celebrated at Lenzburg Castle. Many who attended still remember the former Federal Councillor Nello Celio dancing with the beautiful Italian film star Elsa Martinelli. At the beginning, Hayek also sometimes invited the employees home to his villa in Meisterschwanden. Yet soon hardly anyone at Hayek Engineering had any glimpse into the boss's private domain. Hayek did not reopen his house to guests until he began to celebrate his successes in the watch industry.

One of the last of these occasions at Lake Hallwil, at which some members of the Hayek Engineering team were also honoured, took place at the beginning of the 1960s. Hayek gave a grand reception to celebrate the visit from the acting Russian Automotive Industry Minister. Hayek Engineering was at that time supposed to be taking

over the planning and construction of the Russian lorry factory on the
Kama river at the foot of the Urals for Mercedes. Yet the celebratory
mood was short-lived. The big contract for this huge complex went
unexpectedly to the USA. However, the ten Hayek employees who
had formally declared themselves willing to move to Kama with their
families for four years were not entirely unhappy about the loss of this
contract. The thought of being trapped in a 'golden cage' in the grey,
communist East gave many of them the jitters.

The contractual conditions at Hayek Engineering were not financially
fantastic. Hayek certainly paid his employees according to the usual
calculations for the industry. Before the legal obligation on pension
funds came into force in 1985, however, there was no retirement
provision, in contrast to the competition. In terms of working time, the
consultancy firm was a special case. Whereas the workload at McKinsey
or KPMG, for instance, was already very flexibly managed, at Hayek
Engineering the 40-hour week applied, although only on paper. In fact,
they worked much more; the working days were extremely long. Most
of the employees in any case lived in the Zurich area, away from their
families. At Friday lunchtime the Germans who lived there during the
week travelled home, and the early return journey had to be made
up for by extra work during the week. Also, only directly productive
time was taken into account. Hayek did not consider travelling time
to clients as working time. This time was not charged to the customer,
though, either.

Travelling time was also not counted when, in 1978, a five-strong
team was sent on three six-week visits to Hyundai International in
South Korea. The return journeys alone with a total travelling time of
around 40 hours corresponded to an entire working week. This was
not the now-famous car firm Hyundai but an engineering firm with
around 12,000 employees that was being run by its President like
a craft enterprise. Hayek was commissioned by the World Bank to
examine its organisational structure. South Korea then was still a poor,
developing country with an authoritarian regime. For the Hayek team
it was a busy assignment that required many sacrifices. But they could
at least hope that their efforts would be rewarded by their employer.

At the end of the year, in fact, especially hard-working employees
were paid a bonus on top of their wages. This bonus was decided
by Hayek alone every November in quiet contemplation. As autumn

approached, individual employees would often try to put themselves in a good light with their boss. Whether someone was in Hayek's good or bad books could change from one month to the next and one week to the next. The only objective criterion for this bonus calculation was the time recorded on the work reports. The hours spent on administrative work between two contracts, like the journey times, did not count for the bonus. So every employee had an interest in taking part in as many projects as possible. However, most of them were in any case extremely interested in doing so because a great deal could be learnt on these contracts.

Several employees were able to take up management positions in very different industries because of the skills and knowledge they had gained with Hayek. Thomas Held, for example, became Director of Avenir Suisse, the Swiss economic think-tank; Walter Grüebler became President of the board of directors at Sika Switzerland, and Marco de Stoppani became Editorial Director at the *NZZ*. At Hayek Engineering itself an actual career was almost unthinkable. There were few possibilities of establishing a profile. Unlike the competitor firms, it was not possible there then – nor is it today – to rise to become a partner and acquire a stake in the company. There has always been a very high staff turnover because of the limited future prospects.

The consultancy firm that was started as a specialist in foundry sector matters gradually became a versatile consulting firm. From 1979 to 1981, the projects ranged from the attempt to devise a plan to reorganise the whole AEG-TV radio group in a few weeks to the development of a corporate plan for a medium-sized jewellery factory in which the two estranged proprietors were threatening to attack each other with a gun.

Finally Hayek succeeded over time in acquiring contracts in Switzerland as well. Certainly, even at the beginning of the 1970s, the consultancy firm was commissioned to carry out a study for the reorganisation of the Swiss radio and television company (SRG). Hayek had to work out proposals for restructuring the administration and reinforcing the SRG general management. On his recommendation, radio and television were combined under the newly created post of a Regional Director, but which later proved not to be very sensible. It was also a rather paradoxical contract. For Hayek, organisational structures have never been all that important. He always says that everything depends on the people who are working in the organisation concerned. 'A bad organisational structure with talented, motivated people functions better than an excellent structure with less talented people.' Hayek did not always make friends with these rather unorthodox statements for a consultant. So SRG remained one of the few Swiss clients for some time.

Bringing the former Federal Councillor Nello Celio onto the board of directors at Hayek Engineering finally contributed a great deal to the better acceptance of the consultancy firm in Switzerland. The Ticino Liberal was elected to join the board of directors of various firms after he left the Federal Council in 1973. With Celio, Hayek gained a good connection to politics and industry. An important commission after that was the review of the Central Services and the governance and decision-making processes of the general management at the Swiss Federal Railways (SBB). Gradually, this consultancy firm also gained a good reputation in Switzerland. The SBB report turned out to be so critical, though, that the general management kept it under wraps for over six months. The report was only published in early 1983, and then only under pressure. The Federal Railways were left with no other choice because the editors of the consumer magazine *Kassensturz* of German Swiss Television had found out about the report through a leak and had already published some parts of it. In his accompanying letter to the SBB, Hayek certainly expressed it very diplomatically: 'The concept of profitability has not yet been recognised throughout the SBB as one of the most key foremost requirements.' Yet the report itself used plain language.

The state of the Federal Railways was at that time, in fact, more than bleak. Until 1970 the management deficiencies were not yet visible. So far, the books had balanced. In the following years, though, the Federal Railways recorded a deficit of 100 million francs. The general management was hopelessly overstretched, stated Hayek's report. There was a lack of system, planning, marketing and control. In the general management meetings, up to 60 per cent of the matters handled were purely administrative. The consultants' analysis of the meeting minutes showed that only 3–5 per cent of the forward-looking business was strategic in nature.

Hayek showed in detail that around 100 million francs could be saved with a targeted exploitation of all the possibilities for reducing and optimising costs. The criticism was also made that marketing was not a matter for the boss. At first the report was not well received by the SBB management. The presentation even led to a clash between Hayek and Pierre Arnold, a member of the SBB board. Usually highly sensitive to criticism, Hayek seems to have quickly forgiven Arnold, since he brought him into his watch group not long afterwards as President of the board of directors. The SBB then fairly quickly drew the conclusions from Hayek's critique. The marketing underwent a review. The Marketing Director, Michel Crippa, was promoted just one year after the publication of the report to be SBB Director-General. He was now the head of the marketing and production department, the renamed traffic department. Hayek formulated around 130 improvement proposals. Most of these recommendations were then implemented.

Hayek's report to the Zurich city administration was a world-first. It was the first time that a city had been investigated by a consultancy firm. Hayek received this 500,000 franc contract not least because, unlike his competitors, he had proved that he was not a zealous job-cutter. 'Our goal is not first and foremost to reduce the city's staff headcount; we mainly want to optimise the city's expenditure and income. That can also be achieved by introducing more rational working procedures, analysing material costs and improving other revenues.'

Unlike McKinsey, for instance, which had triggered a wave of redundancies at Sandoz two years earlier with its overhead value analysis, Hayek did not even assume a specific percentage of downsizing. 'We don't accept any guidelines except that there are no taboo areas and no "sacred cows" for our work.' In this way Hayek managed to reassure the political left and even get them on board. The company analysed all the areas of administration, from rubbish collection to policing to the IT system. The report finally contained around 400 proposals for improvements, but far from all of them were implemented. For Hayek this contract was nonetheless a great success. Even the sceptics realised that such an optimisation analysis did not necessarily have to result in heads rolling.

There were also reports in which Hayek even called for an increase in staff. For example, in the study conducted in 1985 under contract from the Swiss Schools Inspector on the two technical colleges and the five associated institutes, Hayek recommended creating 530 further jobs and increasing expenditure by around 100 million francs for ETH. Hayek warned of a severe technological lag for Switzerland if the Federal Government did not lift the recruitment freeze that also applied in the educational sector. A whole series of further analyses followed, for instance at Basel University, the traffic headquarters, and the media companies Ringier, Edipresse and Tages-Anzeiger. Finally, over 20 years later, Hayek had achieved a breakthrough in consultancy work in Switzerland as well.

3

The Leopard Report – how Hayek Tried to Teach the Army to Make Savings

ICOLAS HAYEK DID NOT create a real furore in Switzerland until his report on the biggest arms deal of all time. The man once said to have had a 'lion's heart' as a schoolchild in Lebanon showed his true strengths in dealing with leopards – more specifically in his survey on the procurement of Leopard 2 tanks. With this report he 'shook up the Swiss establishment', as Hayek said around 20 years ago to Sacha Wigdorovits, then editor of the *SonntagsZeitung*. Hayek had certainly already got people talking one year earlier with his proposal to merge the ASUAG and SSIH watch companies. But this caused a stir primarily in business circles and in the Jura region; elsewhere, the restructuring efforts in the watch industry were not yet a major topic. Besides, it was impossible to foresee whether Hayek's prescriptions for saving the watch industry would finally even be worth anything. There was broad scepticism as to whether this industry actually could be saved before it permanently folded.

Unlike the watch industry, the Leopard 2 involved billions of francs in public money. Every Swiss citizen's pocket was affected by this deal. The study on the procurement of the expensive combat vehicle thus became a testimonial for Hayek Engineering throughout Switzerland. With his bold appraisal of the controversial proposal for the Federal Council, Hayek was able to prove his impartiality and independence in public. His credibility soared.

In certain political and business circles though, he also made enemies. In 1984, the Federal Council had proposed to Parliament at the army's request the procurement of 420 Leopard 2 combat tanks at a cost of 4.3 billion francs. The arms deal was just ready to go for discussion to the Swiss councils. The presentation had already been prepared by the former Liberal head of the Military Department, Georges-André

35

Chevallaz, and now had to be put to Parliament by his Waadtland Party colleague and successor, Federal Councillor Jean-Pascal Delamuraz. In 1984 the Soviet Union was still the great danger for Switzerland's security in the army's threat assessment. The top ranks were firmly convinced that the Red Army might infiltrate central Europe at any moment and overrun Switzerland. Only five years before the fall of the Berlin Wall, with the fragmentation process already emerging in the communist East, the officers were getting their soldiers psyched up for this scenario in the exercises. This assessment was also firmly rooted in the minds of most of the population. The political climate meant that the generals' wishes for new and better weapons were generally waved through Parliament without much debate. Anyone who questioned this defence policy ran the risk of being ostracised along with anti-militarists and pro-communists.

Yet the increasingly precarious financial position of the Federal Government created a new situation. The Federal Government was seriously in debt. To make some savings, the Council of States was being forced to cut back the project to 380 combat vehicles. The idea of this procurement proposed by the Federal Council was, however, not itself fundamentally questioned by Parliament. The politicians blindly trusted the costings that were provided by the Contraves, the Bührle subsidiary. The version slightly curtailed by the Council of States planned though that the Swiss arms company Contraves in partnership with some other firms would produce 345 combat tanks under licence and that the Federal Government would buy 35 more tanks directly from the German manufacturer Krauss-Maffei. Even this reduced arms programme now still seemed much too costly to Helmut Hubacher, the Swiss Social Democratic Party (SP) President, National Councillor and member of the National Council's military committee. Hubacher phoned Hans-Jochen Vogel, then Chairman of the Social Democratic Party (SPD) parliamentary party in the German Bundestag, and enquired how much the German army had paid for this tank at the time. The Germans had of course bought their combat vehicles directly from the firm Krauss-Maffei, who had developed this model. Vogel proposed to Hubacher a meeting with the military politicians and experts in his party, since he could not just drum up this calculation on the phone.

So a few days later the SP President travelled with his comrade Fritz Reimann to Bonn. The meeting took place at the Friedrich-Ebert Foundation, the SPD's think-tank. 'We talked till one o'clock in the morning', Hubacher recalls. One of those present was a general who was close to the SPD. Hubacher relates that he nearly fell off his chair when he discovered that the Germans had only paid half the amount that the Federal Council had agreed with the Swiss arms industry. Following the explanations from his German comrade, he reached the conclusion that Contraves had obviously ripped off the Federal Council.

Parliament had not exercised its controlling function. The committee responsible on the Council of States had failed to give proper scrutiny to the deal struck behind closed doors. Not a single person on the committee dared to make a critical remark. No one wanted to risk being sent into the electoral wilderness as a pro-communist. Also, no one wanted to be criticised for putting Swiss jobs at risk by purchasing ready-made goods from the German company Krauss-Maffei, for in a manufacture under licence 500 smaller Swiss firms in addition to Contraves could count on getting contracts as suppliers.

However, Hubacher reached the conviction in his visit to Bonn that the jobs argument did not hold in this case. Furthermore, the Social Democrats were putting the interests of taxpayers in the foreground here. After all this concerned several billion francs. As soon as he got back to Switzerland, Hubacher phoned Nicolas Hayek. At that time he knew the firm only by name but he had discovered in Germany that the consultancy firm had successfully handled a series of contracts in heavy industry there. Hayek was clearly surprised by the SP President's phone call – and pleased: 'I'm delighted that a Swiss politician should be asking my advice as a simple citizen.' Hubacher was given an appointment at Hayek Engineering in Zurich the very next day. When he saw the photos of the many clients with well-known names from Germany in the offices there, he was amazed. This strengthened his conviction that he had taken his matter to the right place.

There was also a good chemistry between Hubacher and Hayek from the outset. Hayek promised Hubacher that he would communicate to him within a few days in a first-glance assessment what he thought of the arms deal. Just three days later he rang him up: 'This is an outright scandal! The price the Federal Council wants to pay Contraves for these tanks is totally extortionate. The figures you have received

from the German SPD are right down to the last mark and pfennig.'
Only then did Hubacher fully realise that he was about to launch a
political bombshell.

This was, of course, a scoop in the making, not only for politicians on
the left but also for the media. It was only a question of time before the
information was passed to journalists. In fact, several newspapers were
writing about the Bern 'financial scandal' just one day after Hubacher's
phone call to Hayek. Hubacher realised that critical coverage alone
could not help him very much. The wily tactician and strategist also
knew that the SP, traditionally regarded as critical of the military,
would never be able to rectify this arms project all on its own. He
considered who might be a possible partner in an alliance. He saw
Adolf Ogi, then President of the Swiss People's Party (SVP) and later a
member of the Federal Council, as a potential partner who was above
suspicion. At that time the SVP was pursuing a centrist middle-class
course. Christoph Blocher was certainly already known as a successful
businessman, but as a politician he did not have much influence on
the Swiss situation as a whole. The majority of the party followed the
tradition of its predecessor, the BGB, the party of farmers, tradespeople
and citizens. The nationalistic and anti-foreign circles at that time
mainly found their home in the Swiss Democrats (SD).

The SVP President Adolf Ogi therefore appeared as a possible partner
also because the forthright highlander from Bern did not have any
fears of political contact. The affable and consensual politician had
already cultivated good contacts beyond the party boundaries. He got
on well with Hubacher, if not politically, then certainly at a human
level. The two of them reached an agreement. This enabled Hubacher
to break through the usual middle-class antagonistic stance towards
the SP in army matters. And with the critical attitude towards the
Leopard procurement, Ogi could present the SVP as the prudent representative of taxpayers' interests in relation to the rival middle-class
parties the FDP and the Christian Democratic People's Party (CVP). For
Ogi also experienced great doubts about this billion-franc tanks deal.
Above all, he feared that the presentation in the Federal Council version
might provoke the left-wing politicians to an arms referendum. So,
together with three SVP parliamentarians, Ogi wrote a letter to Federal
Councillor Jean-Pascal Delamuraz, head of the Military Department. In
it he expressed the suspicion that the Swiss industrial firms concerned,

primarily Contraves, had factored in excessively high profit margins: 'With regard to ... the size of the project it seems to the undersigned SVP members of the military committees that a detailed cost audit of the plan by an external company that is independent in this matter is an absolute necessity', Ogi wrote.

It was the first time that the SVP had questioned an arms programme. This letter did not make any mention of Hayek Engineering, for the introduction of the Zurich consultancy firm had one major snag: the company was still almost unknown to parliamentarians at the time. And among the few Federal politicians who knew Nicolas Hayek, vague prejudices still prevailed. 'His origins and his unconventional, rather showy behaviour put some people on the defensive', recalls one former prominent parliamentarian. The SVP brought some other firms into the discussion, such as Kienbaum and McKinsey. The Zurich SVP in particular expressed the critical view that Hayek was insufficiently serious. Against the tanks procurement and the army, according to a press release from the Zurich cantonal party, there was forming 'a peculiar alliance between a contract-hungry and publicity-happy management consultant with sensationalist journalists and left-wing politicians who want to prepare the way for their arms referendum'. There was a 'strange triangular relationship in the tanks procurement between the SP, Hayek and Ringier'. But Federal Councillor Jean-Pascal Delamuraz, who later became a good friend of Hayek, was also initially opposed. He asked Hubacher whether he really believed that Hayek was the right man to conduct such a survey.

The SP President encountered a broad oppositional stance in Parliament, despite the alliance with Adolf Ogi. Kaspar Villiger, who was later elected to the Federal Council, finally suggested the compromise solution of bringing in the firm Revisuisse as well as the commission to Hayek. This firm should prepare an accompanying study. Yet Hayek's opponents did not give in so quickly. They imposed some conditions to which they thought Hayek would never agree. François Jeanneret, leader of the Liberal Party in Parliament, demanded that Hayek Engineering should have their survey on the Federal Councillor's desk within four weeks. Hubacher replied that this was a totally unrealistic suggestion because Hayek was then on holiday at his villa in Cap d'Antibes in the South of France. Jeanneret immediately tried to suggest that this indicated a bias. 'Hayek is probably also in the

Socialist party if you have that much information'. Yet the Liberal had underestimated Hayek's flexibility. He immediately replied to Hubacher from his holiday home: 'I will prepare this survey for you as requested in four weeks.'

Hayek very quickly summoned together 14 engineers, production specialists, industrial organisational and cost experts and project managers. Under his direction the consultancy firm, together with Revisuisse, delivered a report of around 200 pages to Martin Bundi, SP National Councillor and President of the National Council's military committee. That cost the Federal Government 70,000 francs – a paltry sum compared with the billion-franc deal that was under discussion. The sum was also surprisingly small considering that Hayek at that time generally charged his clients 2,400 francs per day for his own work and 1,200 for his engineers.

A numbered copy of the survey was delivered by courier at home to each of the 23 members of the military committee on 9 November 1984. Every page of the report was marked 'confidential'. Yet two days later the survey's findings were already in the *Sonntagsblick* under the headline '700 million could be saved'. Hubacher, who had copy number 16, was the person immediately suspected in the military committee of having betrayed the secret. Jeanneret immediately demanded that all the committee members swear that they had treated their report confidentially. Hubacher did not want the suspicion of the indiscretion to hang over him. He asked Hayek how many reports had been distributed. There were 34, so eleven more than the number of committee members. So Hayek had rather relieved Hubacher of the suspicion of having committed an indiscretion. The information could also have been leaked by someone outside the committee.

The Hayek report was a sensation. With the consultant's usual highly diplomatic tone, the survey was extremely embarrassing for the Military Department. It made crystal-clear that the generals had in fact been led up the garden path by the firm Contraves. The prices of the tenders were not adequately secured and would have enabled the company to make colossal further demands after fulfilling the contract. 'If we know how dynamically and efficiently the most experienced teams at Krauss-Maffei, Contraves and Rheinmetall operate in the tough market of international defence equipment, we can see how overstretched the GRD team [military department group for arms services] appears under the given structure', states the Hayek report. In their final recommendations, the consultants suggested that the Federal Council create an independent project management to professionalise the execution of the project. For Contraves had a firm grip on the Military Department with this contract. In the text of the contract, the consortium firms were even guaranteed a ban on competition. The competition was to be strictly eliminated in favour of the Swiss suppliers. It ensured that the federally owned construction workshop Thun was not allowed to get any glimpse of the pricing. And the high point of this oppressive contract: the armaments services group was forbidden to make any contact with the consortium members. All the conversations had to go through Contraves. A few people in the Military Department might suddenly yet have realised that dishonest methods were being used here!

Against the construction under licence proposed by the Federal Council at the price of 3.4 billion francs and the direct purchase from Krauss-Maffei, Hayek calculated a potential cost saving of 741 million francs. Instead of the 9 million francs demanded by Contraves, a tank from Krauss-Maffei warehouse would cost only 7 million. For the oscilloscope of the aiming device, for example, Contraves calculated a price of 21,000 francs. Hayek pointed out that a comparable device in Germany cost only around 1,800 francs – not even one tenth of that amount. Hayek also had serious doubts as to whether one kilogramme of hexagon bolts actually had to cost as much as 220 francs.

For these reasons the consultant argued for a direct off-the-shelf purchase from Krauss-Maffei. The advantages were also obvious for other reasons, as the Hayek report stated:

> Krauss-Maffei is booked up till the end of March 1986; there are no further orders. In such a situation follow-up orders can be advantageously negotiated. Krauss-Maffei has amortised its production infrastructure with the few thousand Leopard tanks supplied to the German army and the Dutch army. Every follow-up order brings unanticipated additional revenues, and in a written-down position at favourable prices. EMD [today VBS] could thereby save at least a further 700 million francs, more likely one billion. I consider it more sensible to finance future investments with the money saved than to construct a production structure for 345 tanks with the licensing. The anticipated gain in skills with the manufacture under licence is overestimated. Also, there will never be a tank industry in Switzerland that could profit from the licensing.

The jobs argument that was used for the Swiss manufacture under licence mainly by the Liberals had thus also been refuted by Hayek, for his assessment that tank construction had no future in Switzerland was supported, of course, by his experiences in heavy industry. It was already foreseeable, then, that after the contract ended in 1993 there would be no need for more combat vehicles, regardless of the military threat situation.

After the military committee had learnt of the Leopard report, Hayek spent around six hours explaining himself to the parliamentarians. Civil defence serviceman Hayek impressively demonstrated to them that the generals had bungled this procurement project. The harsh criticism was not to everyone's taste and Hayek was fiercely attacked in the committee. 'It is unbelievable, what we are having to take from Hayek', complained FDP National Councillor Geneviève Aubry. Especially from the Liberals, Hayek reaped much criticism. But the SVP National Councillor Christoph Blocher also fiercely attacked Hayek and called him a left-wing anti-militarist. Hayek obviously did not care whether Switzerland possessed adequate means of defence against possible attackers. Various parliamentarians also pointed to the accompanying report by Revisuisse, which diverged from Hayek's findings in a few respects. So they complained that the cost estimate per productive working hour stated in Hayek's report was too high in comparison with similar industries. In the view of the Revisuisse experts, the cost estimates contained in the Federal Council presentation corresponded in every case to the usual estimates.

Here, now, there was an allegation and a counter-allegation. For Contraves had not allowed the two consultancy firms to see all the bases for their calculations – allegedly on competition grounds. For outsiders – which included the members of parliament – these statements could not therefore be tested. Both the NZZ and the Tages-Anzeiger pointed to various contradictions between the two studies. Hayek suddenly had to fear for his reputation. He retaliated in the Tages-Anzeiger with a counter-statement: 'There can be no talk of a battle between Revisuisse and Hayek because the two partners had different tasks in the project run by Hayek.'

Nevertheless, the diversionary tactic with the Revisuisse report proved effective. Just before Christmas, the National Council still approved their gift of some tanks for the army leaders. Hayek's recommendation to buy the tanks directly from Krauss-Maffei, to save around 1 billion francs, was not followed. Hayek certainly says in his interview with the *NZZ* editor Friedemann Bartu that appeared in book form: 'Ultimately, though, the solution that I had proposed was then chosen.' In fact, the exact opposite was the case. Most of the tanks were not bought from Krauss-Maffei but recreated in Switzerland under licence. However, the Hayek report still led to the Military Department having to go over the books again with the draft contract negotiated with Contraves. Also, the Federal Government's funding obligation was then tied to a series of conditions. A few savings were thus achieved with the replacement parts and ammunition. Admittedly, these were only in the region of a few thousand million francs and were ultimately swallowed up by inflation. On one key point, however, Hayek's recommendation was fulfilled: the Military Department was required to create an independent project management in order to professionalise the execution of the tank deal. Not only with the Leopard, but also for the arms funding that followed, the conclusions were drawn from the advice.

By auditing the most expensive arms deal in the country's history, Nicolas Hayek had now finally been able to make his mark as a competent and critical consultant in Switzerland as well. His prognosis then, that tank production in Switzerland would never become an industry of the future, already seems almost visionary. For just five years after the last Leopard rolled off the production line, around half of these combat vehicles were mothballed as a result of the break-up of the communist Eastern bloc. After the review of the military threat assessment, they were deactivated by the army and, protected against corrosion, placed in massive air-conditioned halls. So the arms deal later turned out also in this respect to have been completely overplayed. There was also no more talk of any knowledge transfer for this production under licence.

For Hayek, this contract had some repercussions: after this episode the arms company Oerlikon-Bührle cancelled its rental contract with Hayek Engineering at Dreikönigstrasse in Zurich. This cannot have worried Hayek because office space was always easy to rent out in Zurich city centre. Hayek had known from the outset that he would not only make friends with this contract: 'I am not afraid of losing contracts with my survey. On the contrary: with it I am gaining new contracts', he told Hubacher, and invited him to a meal at the Hotel

Bellevue in Bern. 'It was really pleasant to work with him', Hubacher recalls. The fact that as a management consultant he was able to acquire the respect of left-wing politicians as well as others may certainly have helped Hayek to win further public contracts with political relevance.

Hubacher later consulted Hayek once again, in fact on the procurement of the FA18 fighter plane. He met him in Biel at his watch group headquarters. Hayek had in personal conversation made some highly critical comments on this loan, too. When Hubacher said goodbye to Hayek, Hayek called over to his secretary: 'Mr Hubacher is sending some more signature sheets for the anti-FA18 initiative'. Whether Hayek then actually signed this petition himself remains his secret. But he has never made a secret of his critical attitude towards the military.

4

Ticking Faster than the Rest – the Decline and Rescue of the Watch Industry

ALMOST IN PARALLEL WITH his investigation of the Leopard proposals, Hayek was working on the reorganisation of the two watch companies SSIH and ASUAG. His consultancy firm obtained these two contracts out of the blue. The watch industry was totally new ground for the Zurich firm. Until then, no Hayek consultant had ever had any dealings with this industry. The request for these surveys came not from the watch companies themselves but from their creditor banks, under whose guardianship both groups had actually stood since the early 1980s. The Union Bank of Switzerland and the Swiss Bank Corporation in particular followed the decline of the two largest watch firms with great unease. The two major banks that later amalgamated as UBS had issued large loans and thus had a great deal to lose. Their representatives even occasionally exercised the right to attend the board of directors' meetings at the two companies as 'guests', although they had no formal position there at all. So they had to watch at the closest proximity as the management boards kept heedlessly muddling along and both companies headed ever deeper into the mire. Both at the Swiss Bank Corporation and at the Union Bank the view was being expressed in the board of directors and the head office that the watch companies should be allowed to fail because there was no future for them. It was feared that the companies might become a bottomless pit.

To explain how this catastrophe came about, a short overview of the history of the Swiss watch industry is required, for this decline came as a great surprise to most observers since the Swiss watch industry had long been world-famous for its inventiveness and innovative spirit. The firm Vacheron & Constantin, for example, was already working in the nineteenth century with tool machines that enabled the tools to be interchanged so that large batches could be produced. The Vacheron & Constantin system had deeply impressed even the critic of capitalism, Karl Marx, who mentioned the watch firm in his major work *Das Kapital*. The watch manufacturers were one of the first economic sectors to make the transition from craft to industry and create an army of wage earners.

The Swiss watch industry began to emerge in the eighteenth and nineteenth centuries. Huguenots who had fled from France under Louis XIV to Switzerland on religious grounds created a flourishing watchmaking trade. In 1845, Antoni Norbert Patek de Prawdzic and Jean Adrien Philippe together founded the high-end brand Patek Philippe. In Calvinist Geneva, the refugees were forbidden to practise their former trade of jewellery-making. The narrow-minded reformers considered jewellery a superfluous luxury: glittering trinkets only spoilt the populace. The refugees from the western neighbouring country therefore fell back on a related craft, namely producing watches.

The art of watchmaking spread rapidly from Geneva across the whole arc of the Jura from the Vallée de Joux through La-Chaux-de-Fonds to Grenchen. A monoculture soon developed in these regions. This precision engineering provided a very good living. Apart from farming, other occupations were only very poorly represented in these regions. In the mid-nineteenth century over 20,000 people were already working in watch production. The small watch movements were often assembled by farm workers as a secondary occupation in their homes in winter when there was little work available in the sparse grassland economy. There was a strict division of labour in the industry. There were manufacturers for the 150–180 different parts (screws, cases, and so on). The etablisseurs (workers or companies who assemble the parts of a watch) bought in these parts, had them assembled by home workers and then distributed them through the specialist trade. Between these two stages, there were cartel-like cooperation agreements that heavily restricted competition.

At first it was mainly expensive luxury watches that were produced in Switzerland. Yet only the rich could afford to buy these elaborately manufactured watches, some of which even then were genuine works of art. During the economic crises of the 1870s and 1880s, Georg Friedrich Roskopf (1813–1889) therefore developed a robust and cheap watch with a simple construction. Since this Roskopf watch, named after its inventor, was also affordable for workers, it was soon colloquially called the 'proletarian's watch'. With this cheap product, the watch industry gained a new, broad stratum of buyers. The opening of this new market very quickly made it the largest sector in the Swiss economy after the textile industry. Production went almost entirely into export and indeed all over the world. The 1930s crisis therefore had much less impact on this geographically diversified industry than on the textile industry based in eastern Switzerland. The sale of cloth and embroidery was concentrated in a few key outlets, and this industry was therefore much more vulnerable than the watch industry.

Despite the relatively comfortable surrounding conditions, the Federal Government took the watch industry under its wing. Other industries that were in difficulty received no assistance. With the justification that any further spread of the economic crisis had to be prevented in Switzerland, ASUAG was founded in 1931 with a financial stake from the Federal Government. The core of the new company was the raw movement producer Ebauches SA. This strategically important company, which manufactured the centrepiece of the watch, became the backbone of the entire industry. As their parent company, ASUAG was explicitly obligated in the statutes to supply all the Swiss watch manufacturers with raw movements and parts. All the previously independent raw movement producers were integrated into the newly formed group for this purpose. A near monopoly arose for the manufacture of watch movements. The new structure of the industry was legally underpinned by a state-sanctioned cartel, the so-called watch statute. This prohibited all firms from exporting abroad chablons (complete sets of unassembled components for a movement) and parts, as well as watchmaking machinery and tools.

Of course, this rule was diametrically opposed to the freedom of trades and crafts that was enshrined in the Federal Constitution. Yet the Federal Council and Parliament were firmly convinced that this would enable them to protect the Swiss watch industry from the upsurge of any foreign competition. This erroneous belief was held until long into the postwar period. The old watch statute was thus superseded in 1951 by the equally protectionist federal decision concerning measures to maintain the Swiss watch industry. The opening and expansion of watch factories was made subject to an authorisation requirement. Such radical anti-competitive regulations never applied in agriculture. The watch industry thus lived for decades under a cheese cover. It was cut off from any air supply, or any competitive pressure.

As a result of intense lobbying by the industry, the watch statute was even extended for ten further years in the 1961 referendum, although the trade was still flourishing. Until the end of the 1960s, the Swiss watch industry was the global leader. Every second watch came from Switzerland. Watch-workers were among the best-paid employees in the country, and their professional pride was correspondingly great. Along with typographers, they belonged to the 'worker aristocracy' of the Swiss trade union movement. Their product was part of Switzerland's calling card abroad. Swiss-made watches embodied Swiss inventiveness, quality, precision and reliability. This gave the whole industry prestige and a correspondingly strong influence domestically as well.

The self-contained manufacturing system that had existed since the 1930s crisis had the effect of a sleeping draught on the industry. The autocratic watch barons did not realise that profound technological changes were occurring on the global markets and that the market needs were changing. Soon Asian manufacturers flooded the markets with cheap electronic watches. This became even easier when an important sales argument – accuracy – lost some force. For the introduction of electronics had now made all watches reasonably accurate. So the industry went into rapid decline at the beginning of the 1970s. By 1975, only every eighth watch sold worldwide was still Swiss-made. This development was all the more serious given that this industry was not only a Swiss flagship but also still the third most important export sector after the chemical and engineering industries.

It did not take long for the decline in the Swiss watch industry to attract great attention abroad, too. The American financial magazine *Business Week* was even predicting its collapse. Such headlines were fatal to its image on the foreign markets. They undermined consumer confidence. Who will buy a watch with a 'loser' image? No one wants to have to reckon with their chosen brand ceasing to exist and losing any available 'after-sales' or repair service. Certainly Switzerland still held a leading position in the luxury watches domain. With Rolex, Patek Philippe and a few other prestige brands, there were still a few bastions of success. However, in the middle and lower price segments Swiss manufacturers were being literally overrun by the competition from the Far East. For now the manufacture and sale of these watches was no longer based on the long-established Swiss skill in precision engineering but on a completely new technology. The watch business was turning into an ordinary volume business.

Worldwide production doubled within ten years to around 300 million units, of which around two thirds were electronic chronometers. Nevertheless, the firms in La Chaux-de-Fonds, Biel and Grenchen still restricted themselves to the engineering technology. The watch manufacturers saw no reason to climb down from their high horse. They were still bursting with self-assurance. With the mechanical luxury watches, Switzerland was, after all, still a market leader with a share of almost 90 percent. Yet this development turned out to be a flight into an extremely narrow market niche. The Swiss producers were sitting on the golden pinnacle of the product pyramid and failing to notice as the foundations underneath them were crumbling.

The Swiss watch industry certainly had the possibility then of maintaining or even expanding its leading position. The first quartz watch in the world had already been invented in Neuenburg in 1967 with the Beta 1. The movement developed at the Centre Electronique Horloger in Neuenburg was an electronic watch with hands, so with an analogue display. This technology has prevailed over the digital display, as we know today. Yet the opportunity to implement this ground-breaking innovation in the market in good time was wantonly squandered. On the management floors of the watch companies, there was insufficient interest and understanding of the new technology.

However, the foreign competition kept bringing further innovations on to the market. Many of these new developments were nothing more than gimmicks that finally proved to be one-hit wonders. But they caused serious trouble for the Swiss watch industry. In 1971 the American firm Hamilton launched the first completely electronic watch with the Pulsar. It showed the time with light-emitting diodes (LED). It was anything but a masterpiece. Whenever its wearer wanted to tell the time, he had to press a button first to save the battery. The designer, incidentally, was a Swiss called Neuhaus. The Japanese firm Ricoh soon followed suit and offered an LED watch at a much lower price of 1,000 francs. Then the American firm Timex presented an even cheaper electronic watch for 225 francs. In watch technology everything was in flux. Soon the LED display was replaced by liquid crystal display (LCD) watches. The prices continued to spiral down even further.

The electronic watch was about to put an end to the mechanical watch, the pride of the Swiss watch industry. The days when a movement from Ebauches SA in Grenchen still ticked in every fourth chronometer worldwide were over. It had simply become impossible to keep up with the price competition. The prices per movement fell to a few dollars.

Manufacturers from Hong Kong and Japan flooded the markets with nearly one billion cheap electronic quartz watches. Watches with a digital display comprised two thirds of the global market until the early 1980s. They were cheaper and still more accurate than the mechanical Roskopf watches that were still being produced by the Swiss. The engineering-based Roskopf technology had long been superseded. Low-cost, automated mass production was impossible with this antiquated technology. Furthermore, there was no longer any consumer demand for these watches. Gradually, Switzerland was being pushed into third place as the watch nation by Hong Kong and Japan. Yet in the Swiss watch industry the 'slant-eyed imitators' in the Far East were still being denigratingly mocked. Certainly the Japanese learnt a great deal by observing the Swiss. However, in implementing innovations they worked much more efficiently and economically. The Swiss watch industry should have had the best cards up its sleeve to stay at the top. As well as the Beta 1 developed in Neuenburg, many much more interesting developments slumbered in the drawers at La Chaux-de-Fonds, Neuenburg, Biel and Grenchen, most of which never made it to the point of marketability. Whereas the Japanese went into the markets to take soundings from consumers, the Swiss waited for customers to come to them. For around 200 years they had grown used to their products more or less selling themselves.

There is a fine example that nicely illustrates this passivity. Representatives from the trade association Fédération Horlogère (FH) and the big watch firms would await the arrival of a Chinese buying delegation every year at Kloten airport. The visit from the Chinese almost had a ritual status. When, on one such occasion, the high-ranking officials in the green Mao costume sent by the provincial governments bought fewer watches than the previous year, this certainly caused the Swiss some irritation. However, they did not consider what the reasons might be. Then suddenly came the great shock: in 1981 the Chinese cancelled all their orders on cost-saving grounds.

It should have been foreseeable that no further progress was possible on this path. The economic conditions worsened noticeably for Switzerland as a high-wage country. The franc was growing ever stronger and the dollar was continuing to weaken. This greatly compounded the price disadvantage of Swiss watches in foreign markets. For almost 100 per cent of the costs at the manufacturing site accrued in hard Swiss francs, while most of the revenue on the foreign markets was in soft dollars. With their currency pegged to the US dollar, the Hong Kong Chinese gained another competitive advantage in addition to the technological advances. Furthermore, the strong exchange rate fluctuations of the Swiss export economy made any reliable calculation or stable pricing policy enormously difficult.

In the economic slump of the early 1970s almost the whole Swiss export industry complained that business was going badly. Whereas most other sectors of the Swiss economy tried to adapt to the new conditions, the management boards at the two watch companies ASUAG and SSIH instead began to lament long and loud about the unfavourable surrounding conditions. The recession had only brought to light the long-standing underlying weaknesses of the industry. The reasons for the decline were mainly of their own making. Unlike the vertically structured, entrepreneurially run Japanese companies Citizen and Seiko, the two Swiss watch companies were bureaucratic organisations. Neither SSIH nor ASUAG, which actually should have taken a leading role, had a clear strategy. Their overstaffed boards of directors operated like parliaments. Some of the well-known figures on them concentrated much more on lobbying in the Federal government than on their own tasks as supervisory and monitoring bodies. Because of the continually strengthening franc, SSIH even asked the Federal Council and the Swiss National Bank to split the exchange rate. This was echoed by Peter Renggli, President of the board of directors at ASUAG: 'If the dollar drops to two francs, the state must take steps.' Apart from the luxury brands in Geneva, the situation in the industry seemed increasingly hopeless. Both Omega and Tissot, the two cornerstones of SSIH, and Longines, which belonged to the ASUAG group, were losing more and more ground.

Then came the first mass redundancies. And the Federal Government was back again with its protecting arm. Bern established a law on financial assistance for economically threatened regions, the so-called Bonny Decree. The architect of this bill was the Director of BIGA (Bundesamt für Industrie, Gewerbe und Arbeit, Federal Office for Industry, Trade and Labour), Jean-Pierre Bonny. He sat on the ASUAG board of directors as the federal representative. So the watch industry had a spokesman in the highest position in the Federal Administration. Bonny later campaigned as a Liberal National Councillor for an extension of the validity term of this law in a slightly modified form. Also the connection between Bern and the trade association Fédération Horlogère worked extremely well. FH President Gérard Bauer was a former diplomat. So for the effective representation of his interests, he knew the workings of the Bern administration inside out.

Yet this corruption network could not do very much to help the watch industry in the long run. The turnovers and profits still sank massively despite the state's dispensations. One BIGA study kept under lock and key at the Bundesgasse in Bern anticipated the worst. The Federal Office that was especially closely linked with the industry in the figure of Bonny actually wanted to conceal the bleak future prospects. As editor of the Swiss News Agency (SDA), I ensured that the report reached the public. For this Bonny later tried to get me dismissed from my post by the SDA Director Georges Duplain. The anticipated scenario was that the number of employees would fall in the coming years from 90,000 to 30,000. And that is exactly what happened. By 1985, half the watch firms had closed their gates and the number of employees had dropped to one third of the original number.

The situation looked worst at SSIH. The finished watches company had large debts at over 30 banks. A series of doctors had already tried to force their prescriptions on the company. After a former manager from the tobacco multinational Philip Morris had unsuccessfully thrown in the towel, the trading group Siber Hegner from the Brandt and Tissot families took over the helm. McKinsey was also consulted on one occasion. Yet at Omega the warehouses were still piling up with unsaleable expensive watches. They did not fit the market trend and they were too expensive. In 1980 the Omega-Tissot group, as SSIH was also known, recorded a loss of over 160 million francs. The six house banks (Union Bank of Switzerland, Swiss Bank Corporation,

Swiss Credit, the People's Bank, Cantonal Bank of Bern and Cantonal Bank of Neuchâtel) immediately granted the company a bridging loan to secure its solvency and proposed a reorganisation plan. However, this move did not generate universal love in return. Then the Union Bank, as the house bank, exercised strong pressure and presented the remaining creditors with the alternative of either taking part in the reorganisation or instead having to write off all their assets. When one pension fund of one large Swiss company proved recalcitrant, Peter Gross, Director-General of the Union Bank, threatened to make this public. That had an impact.

The crucial general meeting took place on 16 June. The family shareholders certainly continued to be obstructive. The mood was extremely heated. At the turbulent meeting, insults such as *salaud* (bastard) and *imbécile* (idiot) were flung around. Yet finally the majority accepted the inevitable and the reorganisation was approved. Gross was chosen as the new President of the board of directors. As a first step, the creditors abandoned demands that amounted to a total sum of 100 million francs. At the same time the share capital was slashed to 5 per cent of the nominal value. In other words, the shareholders finally renounced their money. At the same time the banks created new share capital by converting their demands to equity. The creditor banks thus became the dominant shareholders. The driving force behind this reorganisation plan, as well as Peter Gross of the Union Bank, was Walter Frehner from the Bank Corporation.

The watch industry was still burdening the banks with a massive cluster risk. With the SSIH, however, it was not only a matter of these outstanding demands. With the rescue operation, they were also much more concerned to prevent a chain reaction. If SSIH went bankrupt, it would in fact have taken a whole series of other corporate clients and so also more debtors of the banks down with it. There was also a danger that Omega, the strongest and most world-famous brand, would be wiped out altogether. That would have had a catastrophic effect on the entire industry. Yet there was still no sign of a change in trend. The order book situation at SSIH worsened visibly, and with it also the profit situation. Now the management boards of the financial institutions were gradually losing patience. The Union Bank and the other banks to which SSIH was in debt did not want to waste any more time. The proponents of a radical solution were increasingly gaining the upper hand.

However, Peter Gross warned against any hasty steps. He suggested first undertaking an analysis of the situation before coming to any decisions with far-reaching consequences. The top management of the Union Bank agreed. The major bank put out some feelers for various possible interested parties in this commission. One of those under discussion was Hayek Engineering. In March 1981, Gross informed the board of directors at SSIH that he was considering commissioning external consultants to conduct a problem analysis. The board had little choice but to agree, since these gentlemen were up to their necks in water. Without the assistance from the banks, they were lost anyway.

On a Tuesday at 4.00 p.m. after the meeting of the SSIH board of directors, Gross phoned Nicolas Hayek in Zurich and asked him if he would be able to take on this commission if necessary. Hayek expressed strong interest. Just three hours later he was at SSIH in Biel to discuss the matter with Gross and the Director-General, Ulrich Doenz. Afterwards Hayek and Gross went to a restaurant in the nearby surroundings of Biel for an evening meal. There they scribbled down together the most important parts of the commission on the back of the menu.

The very next day Hayek called in his Vice-Director Jochem Thieme and told him about his visit to Biel:

> I did not completely understand everything Doenz, the Director, told me. There is a fairly confused situation in this firm. One thing was immediately clear to me though: this watch group has serious problems. Go over there tomorrow. I've already told them to expect you. See what we can do and draft a work proposal.

A few days later Gross had an offer on the table. The banker was deeply impressed by this consultant's flexibility. To him it was obvious that Hayek was the right man for the job. Gross gave him the contract.

Hayek then sent Thieme to Biel again, this time for longer. Thieme moved into an office at Omega at 96 Jakob-Stämpfli-Strasse and began with a few employees to get an operational analysis under way. The Hayek people entered a world that was totally alien to them. The consultants who travelled from Zurich found that most of their discussion partners spoke only French. Also, when they asked the staff questions, specialist terms were thrown at them such as *étanche* (waterproof), and *ébauches* (raw movements), which they had never heard before. Instead of the previous large, noise-filled factory buildings with hissing furnaces, they now moved around in quiet, meticulously clean, watch workshops with hardly a speck of dust on the workbenches. Certainly, here as elsewhere, they began by analysing the manufacturing costs. They went into the smallest details of Omega, as the group's most important brand. They became increasingly aware that the conditions in this industry were fundamentally different from those in heavy industry. The consumer goods industry not only had a totally different clientele but also a completely different cost structure.

A few weeks later, Thieme drove back to Zurich and gave Hayek a preliminary report. Explaining the completely new situation to Hayek required some effort of clarification. The lever had to be applied there in a completely different position from that in German heavy industry. Certainly, as in many other firms, especially in the area of management and administration, a great deal more money could be saved at this watch firm, too. However, Thieme identified the greatest need for action in the products policy, marketing and distribution. Change was also urgently needed in the outdated company culture. This was primarily a matter of leadership and therefore a personnel problem.

Hayek's consultants encountered completely fossilised structures and antiquated ways of thinking in the group. Despite the poor state of business, the management team at the Omega-Tissot group had still not yet noticed that their business-as-usual policy would inevitably lead to doom. Only now, when the house banks sent external consultants into the company and applied increasing pressure, did they slowly begin to realise the gravity of the situation.

But the SSIH was not the only watch company with serious problems by a long way. In the Jura region at that time a joke went round at the regular tables: 'What's the difference between SSIH and ASUAG?' The answer: 'A year.' People were expecting that just one year after SSIH, ASUAG would also have to be reorganised by the banks. And that is what happened.

Very soon the ASUAG-Ebauches group also had to introduce short-time working for their 13,500 employees because of the bad order situation. There were also redundancies in many of 100 or so manufacturing sites. For the employees who had worked all their lives in the watch industry, that was a disaster. In the upper Jura region, there were only a few similarly attractive jobs outside the watch industry. Also, in the Bern canton, for example, there was not yet any compulsory unemployment insurance. Only half the employees who were made redundant or had their hours cut were insured. The dramatic erosion of the income stream, however, made such drastic measures unavoidable. The trade unions took note of this in a resigned way and just kept trying to get the best out of the difficult situation for their members. Meanwhile it became clear to everyone that things could not continue as before. All the alarm bells were sounding. In the ASUAG group accounting, which was first consolidated in 1981/1982, an astronomical consolidated loss of 200 million francs was identified.

After Hayek Engineering had already identified the weaknesses at SSIH and done some truly impressive work, the banks commissioned the Zurich consultant in early 1982 to conduct an analysis of ASUAG as well. For the consultancy firm, that was an even bigger undertaking. Not only the finished watch brands Longines, Rado, Certina and Mido, but also the manufacturers of the movements and parts for the company had to be investigated. More than ten Hayek employees were therefore temporarily assigned for one year. In parallel, the creditor banks drove forward the gradual reorganisation of the company based on the consultants' recommendations. In this case, too, a capital reduction was planned. Like the other shareholders, the Federal Government had to write off most of its 8 per cent stake.

The Hayek Engineering report, entitled 'Analysis and Optimisation of the Group's Management Structure', culminated in the recommendation to sack the entire management. The group management was replaced by a five-strong steering committee (STEA). As well as the bank representatives and selected experts, Ernst Thomke sat on this board. As the person responsible for the movements manufacturing, he was one of the few established watch managers who did not have to be criticised for any mistakes. To the contrary, Thomke had quickly recognised the signs of the times and acted within his area of responsibility. Hayek and his colleague Jochem Thieme also had advisory roles on the steering committee. This steering committee was granted wide-ranging special powers.

In autumn 1982, the crucial meeting took place at the Victoria Jungfrau hotel in Interlaken. The conversations were held behind closed doors from Friday evening till long into the Sunday night. At this marathon meeting, the future course was set for the core of the Swiss watch industry. The steering committee decided, on Hayek's advice, to merge the two companies SSIH and ASUAG. There were many common points between the two groups, and there was a lot of duplication. Both companies had their own movements production. However, at the same time the two companies also had a fundamentally different corporate culture. Whereas, for example, at ASUAG, Swiss German was predominantly spoken, at the finished watch producer SSIH, French dominated. The merger was to be completed quickly because a bankruptcy petition had already been filed for ASUAG. The collapse of this leading movements producer would probably have spelt the end for the financially and technologically independent Swiss watch industry.

The merger decision was not announced, though, until May the following year when Hayek Engineering published its keenly awaited final report. At that time almost no one in Switzerland still believed the crisis-stricken companies could be saved. Yet the key message of Hayek's report suddenly allowed a faint hope to emerge. Hayek's final conclusions were clear: the number one weakness was the lack of a consistent branding policy; the second was the under-automation of production. The report at least ended on an optimistic note. The diagnosis was that the Swiss watch industry still had great future potential. When Hayek gave his verbal commentary on his analysis, he went one step further and called the Swiss watch industry a 'slumbering leviathan'.

On Hayek's recommendation, the newly formed company was split into three parts: finished watches, parts and components, as well as the division for diversified industrial products. The francophone head of Galenica, François Milliet, became the President. Thomke joined the board of directors, and was responsible for finished watches as well as the movements division. In summer 1984, the NZZ described Thomke as the leading director at ASUAG/SSIH. Hayek also already exercised a strong influence on the company policies at this point. However, it was still the banks that held sway as the dominant shareholders and creditors.

However, they now broadly followed Hayek's recommendations. He suggested a concentration of personnel and a purge of the management structure. This should restore competitiveness and allow the lost market shares to be regained in the foreign markets. ASUAG became the umbrella holding company and SSIH was incorporated into it. To carry out all these reorganisation measures, however, some further payments from the banks were necessary. These, primarily the Union Bank, the Bank Corporation, the Cantonal Bank of Bern and the People's Bank, had poured in around one billion francs in total for the reorganisation. This money was used partly to conceal losses and partly as new risk capital. For this the banks had to draw on their providently built-up reserves. Of course, they hoped to be able to recover some of it in the form of dividends and proceeds from a subsequent sale of their stake. Even at the announcement of the merger of SSIH and ASUAG the pool banks had made it clear that they did not want to have their stakes on their balance sheets in the long term. First, they did not consider industrial holdings as their task. And second, they still took a highly sceptical view of the position of the watch industry. The fact that they had only narrowly avoided selling off Omega as the group's best-known brand to the Japanese for 400 million francs plus licensing fees shows how little confidence they had in the company's future prospects. However, Hayek urgently advised them against such a step. That would have practically cut the head off the company.

Hayek's assessment proved to be right. Just one year after the merger, the new watch company was slowly turning around. After a loss-making year, for the first time a small operating profit was in prospect for 1984. Hayek felt that this confirmed his judgement. Yet he was not then thinking about entering the watch business himself. This followed rather by chance. In summer 1984, he met Peter Gross for lunch. The two of them chatted about everything under the sun. Hayek mentioned in passing to the banker that he wanted to invest some of his capital in an industrial firm. He had already generated substantial assets of around 200 million francs with his consultancy firm. Hayek asked Gross if he would see if there was any interesting investment for sale among his clients. He was considering acquiring a stake in the high-tech field. Gross stuttered briefly and then burst out: 'But we're both idiots. This new watch company fits with all your ideas! You know it best. Even a due diligence test would be unnecessary.' Gross suggested to Hayek that he buy the majority shareholding from the banks. After all, they had long wanted to get rid of the hot potato they had taken up a few years earlier as soon as possible. Gross finally saw an opportunity after all the aggravation that he had experienced with this reorganisation exercise to bring the whole story to a crowning conclusion.

However, Hayek did not want to commit himself immediately. He pondered this proposal for several days and weighed up all the pros and cons. Instinctively, he must have sensed that the opportunity of a lifetime had arrived for him. He saw a way of fulfilling a long-cherished wish finally to become an industrialist himself. As a consultant, he may always have been slightly bothered by the image of the powerless eunuch. So he finally put the idea for discussion to a board of directors' meeting at Hayek Engineering. Among those present at this meeting were his wife Marianne, and former Federal Councillor Nello Celio. But, to Hayek's disappointment, all the board directors voted against his proposal. He should keep well away from the economically sensitive watch industry. It was precisely its independence that constituted Hayek Engineering's special strength. Through the financial connection to the watch industry this would be lost. Yet Hayek decided to proceed all the same, though not with the consultancy firm's money but with his own private assets. In October 1984 he notified Gross of his interest. He immediately informed his boss, Niklaus Senn. The President of the Union Bank was evidently delighted. 'That is manna from heaven!', he is said to have called out.

By January the following year Hayek had signed an agreement with the financial institutions for an option limited to two years for up to 51 per cent of the share capital. He certainly did not want to put all his eggs in the same basket, but to keep his risk in manageable limits. So he began to look for additional investors, including through newspaper adverts. The first to declare himself ready to acquire a stake was the multibillionaire and important investor Stephan Schmidheiny. Certainly, he was warned at the time by some 'serious representatives of the Swiss economy' against taking on such a risk, Schmidheiny later explained. But the fact that Hayek had been willing to risk his own capital on the accuracy of his recommendations had strongly impressed him. As a first step, the two of them took over a shareholding of 7 per cent each at the beginning of 1985. The news immediately inspired the imagination of the stock exchange. The share price of the company that was now relaunched as SMH (Schweizerische Gesellschaft für

Mikroelektronik und Industrie) rose, despite a zero dividend. Hayek had already indicated at this point that he considered his involvement as a long-term risk investment and he was not seeking quick profits. The speculation drove the price up to 800 million francs in the summer of the same year.

Now Hayek came under some time pressure, for he had decided to become even further involved. He realised that the longer he deferred, the more expensive the business might become. In the second half of August, the time was right. With a consortium of investors, Hayek took over a majority stake of 51 per cent. Hayek and Schmidheiny paid 47 million francs each for their two 17 per cent stakes. For Schmidheiny, this sum was peanuts anyway, while for Hayek it represented around one quarter of his capital at that time. A further 16 per cent of the share capital was taken over by an illustrious group of around a dozen Swiss German investors. With the billionaire Esther Grether (Nivea, Grether's pastilles, and others), Hayek also had a woman on board.

But what his club still lacked was someone from the French-speaking part of the country. For psychological reasons, Hayek felt it was important for the company that also had strong roots in western Switzerland to have a figurehead from this linguistic region. He had been able to convince Pierre Arnold, then still head of the Migros group, to take over the role of President and delegate of the board of directors. He had been required to step down as head of Migros on age grounds. On the SMH board of directors, Arnold replaced François Milliet, who had not got on well with Hayek from the outset. It took Hayek more effort, though, to tie in Arnold as an investor as well. He almost had to get down on his knees to get him to take out a financial stake, Hayek once told me in a personal conversation. Obviously, the former boss of the major distributor had not managed to secure himself a substantial financial cushion there. So he had to borrow 2 million francs to acquire the SMH shares. In retrospect, he could hardly have regretted it. A few years later he was able to sell his shareholding for many times that amount to Hayek and Schmidheiny. They exercised their pre-emptive rights because at the time they wanted to prevent Arnold from selling the shares to the highly controversial property developer Jürg Stäubli, with whom he was friendly.

Hayek was clearly the pack-leader in this pool of investors. He ensured that the consortium was tightly organised and that everyone had to run in the same direction with him. In the pool agreement it was laid down that before any disposal of shares these had to be offered first to consortium members. If no one expressed an interest, the stake could then be sold to a third party but only to someone who was acceptable to the investor group. Hayek retained the fully extensive managerial responsibility. He could exercise the majority vote on the board of directors and towards the management alone and en bloc. He had carefully protected himself against any possible palace revolution in the consortium with a right of veto. Furthermore, Hayek signed a secondary pool agreement with Schmidheiny. In this the eastern Swiss billionaire delegated his voting rights to Hayek. However, at the beginning the two of them had discussions on a weekly basis during important decisions.

Although Hayek was only one of several minority shareholders, he had achieved the feat of becoming the leading figure in the watch company with a series of contractual agreements. Also, he had a powerful information lead over all the other investors, including Schmidheiny. Hayek Engineering had, after all, investigated both SSIH and ASUAG, from which SMH then emerged, in the utmost detail, and so been able to gain valuable insider knowledge. All the important information lay in a drawer at Hayek Engineering in Zurich. Although Hayek did not initially belong to the board of directors and exercised no official role in the company, he was effectively the absolute ruler by virtue of the pool agreement. Not till June 1986 did Hayek take over the presidency and the operational management of the company in a double mandate. Until this point Arnold held office as President of the board of directors. Ernst Thomke was the Director-General with responsibility for the movements production and the entire watch division (Omega, Longines, Tissot, Rado, Mido, Certina, Swiss Timing, and others). Thomke therefore had over 30 per cent of Swiss watch production under his stewardship.

For Hayek, it was all in all a brilliant masterstroke. He celebrated it with an illustrious string of guests at his home in Meisterschwanden. The skies were slightly cloudy around Lake Hallwil, as one of the guests then invited remembers. Yet Hayek had provided a marquee for all eventualities. Federal Councillor Kurt Furgler explained to the guests in a witty speech what SMH meant, namely *sehr moderne Herren* – very modern gentlemen. He also suggested renaming Hayek's place of residence Meisterschwanden 'Meisterkommen' in future.* However, the watch industry was not the only topic of conversation. Hayek's grandson Marc and his BMX races, in which he had just become a Swiss champion, were also talked about at this garden party.

The members of the investor pool present, headed most prominently by Stephan Schmidheiny, also had every reason to celebrate. In total, the dozen or so backers paid around 150 million francs for the majority stake. They had obtained the company for less than half the value it had since reached on the stock exchange. It was an absolute bargain. The analysts at the banks had grossly underestimated the company's future prospects and thus its value.

---

* *Translator's note*: the name 'Meisterschwanden' as two words would mean 'masters or champions disappeared', whereas 'Meisterkommen' would mean that they are coming.

5

Who Invented It?
The Paternity Test for the Swatch

ONLY NOW DID WORK begin in earnest for Hayek. He had to steer his still-shaky watch company onto a long-term successful course. He was certainly able to build on a solid foundation. With the innovative Swatch, the company was already well on its way to regaining the lowest price segment in the global market. When Hayek acquired his financial stake in the ASUAG/SSIH group, the Swatch had already been launched and it was already a successful product. Nevertheless, this watch is now inseparably linked with the figure of Nicolas G. Hayek, the founder and main shareholder of the Swatch Group. A brief overview will therefore now follow to illustrate how this watch came to be developed and when Hayek began to play a critical role in its success story. Hayek has in fact only been called 'Mister Swatch' or the 'Father of the Swatch' in the media since the early 1990s. When this watch first began to make its international breakthrough, Ernst Thomke and his colleague Elmar Mock were still in the glare of publicity. It was only when Thomke left the company in 1991 in the quarrel with Hayek that the history of the Swatch was rewritten.

A key role was played in the invention of this new type of fashion watch by the two engineers Elmar Mock and Jacques Müller. Both were strongly nurtured by Thomke. So in 1988 the legendary lifestyle magazine *Tempo* entitled its profile of Thomke 'Dr Swatch'. The Swatch could certainly never have caused that kind of worldwide sensation if Hayek had not recognised the underlying potential of the two watch companies ASUAG and SSIH and their products. Hayek saved a large section of the industrial fabric of the Swiss watch industry by acquiring his financial stake. By founding SMH and the Swatch Group that later emerged from it, he turned the Swatch into a global brand. 'And yet Hayek had about as much to do with inventing and launching the Swatch as a hippopotamus with impregnating a humming-bird', says an industry insider.

Jochem Thieme, who worked in a managerial post for 15 years in total at Hayek's consultancy firm and was then his closest colleague in the watch sector, told me for the first time in a conversation for this book what really happened then. Thieme was instructed as a project manager by Hayek Engineering to investigate both the watch companies. He himself also wrote large sections of the final report and was therefore a key figure in the reorganisation efforts. 'When Hayek Engineering set about putting ASUAG under the microscope, the Swatch project was already in full swing at the subsidiary company ETA', Thieme says today. Hayek Engineering only in fact completed its overall assessment early in 1983. At the end of 1982, the *NZZ* was still printing the headline 'Waiting for Hayek'. The investigation of ASUAG had recently got well under way. However, by then the Swatch had already been launched. In summer 1983 – a few months after Hayek's report was published – the *NZZ* celebrated the accessory watch with the headline 'Overwhelming success of the Swatch'. In autumn the bombshell then also landed in Germany. And in the Jelmoli department store the shoppers were almost tearing the new watches from each other's hands.

'The Swatch was certainly mentioned in the four volumes of Hayek's final report, each of which was around four to five centimetres thick. Yet the potential and the true significance of this innovation was not yet properly recognised', Thieme explains. At the time this report was published, draft contracts had already been drawn up for marketing the Swatch in several foreign markets. 'The ETA head Ernst Thomke showed us consultants only his extra-thin watch, the Delirium tremens. He kept the Swatch project secret from us for a long time', Thieme remembers.

Another memory: the banks still held sway at the SSIH and ASUAG watch companies until the beginning of September 1985. Hayek only found out about the Swatch project in 1983 at a meeting of the ASUAG steering committee. This took place early in the year at Hayek Engineering in Zurich. The committee met at very short intervals because the banks required all the capital expenditure requests to be approved by the steering committee. The moment thus soon arrived when Thomke needed the go-ahead to continue his project. He was now forced to get the necessary funds granted by this committee. Despite the relatively small sum, the response to Thomke's proposal from the two large bank representatives, Peter Gross and Walter Frehner, was initially anything but positive. 'What kind of nonsense is Thomke dreaming up now?', was the gist of their first reaction. They still at least wanted to give the head of ETA the opportunity to justify his funding request at the next meeting. Their scant knowledge of the industry always made the bankers act very cautiously anyway.

Thomke was annoyed by the hesitation and cumbersomeness of the decision-making process. He sent to the meeting participants' homes a thick parcel with technical drawings, draft contracts and suchlike only on the Friday, at the last minute, before the meeting fixed for Monday. With a reference to the hard-working Sunday in prospect he wished them all – not without a sarcastic undertone – a nice weekend. Thomke inserted a Swatch with an individually made dial into each file. Hayek received a Swatch that depicted a shark (*Haifisch* – HayEck) biting into the corner (*Ecke*) of the ETA building in Grenchen. The watches for the bank representatives were decorated with the money donkey from the children's story by the Brothers Grimm, and Thieme's watch portrayed a mole. Here, too, the reference was easy to understand: as the 'mole' sent from Hayek Engineering, it was Thieme's task to bring to light the weaknesses in the two watch companies SSIH and ASUAG. Neither the bank representatives nor Hayek initially showed much appreciation for this style of humour.

One of the Swatches that Ernst Thomke presented to the SMH steering committee with his funding request in 1983. The watch with the mole on the dial was received by Hayek's employee Jochem Thieme.

Yet Thomke managed to impress the steering committee with his presentation. He promised that the Swatch would be the cheapest and best watch of all time. It would completely change buying behaviour because in future ladies would also buy a Swatch to go with each new jumper. The watch would become a fashion accessory. 'I'll sell people Swatch watches until they're up to their knees in them', he declared. His message was that the Swiss watch industry had to succeed in regaining the lower price segment if it was to save its more expensive prestige brands. To achieve a low-cost production of movements and parts in the finished watches, the largest possible batches and numbers of units were required. However, ASUAG was finding this increasingly difficult to manage. Since the drop in sales, the company had been increasingly forced to export parts, as there was little demand in Switzerland. This meant a substantial proportion of the added value was being lost. For an exported finished watch, the industry realises many times the profit that can be anticipated for a sold raw movement. However, for strategic reasons there was no question of abandoning movements and parts production, as that would have meant a dangerous loss of skill and technological control for the Swiss watch industry. Only by regaining the cheap segment could a majority of the added value be kept in the country. This was the precise significance of the Swatch, as Hayek very quickly recognised. This strategic thinking was the only means of saving the industry that had already been pronounced dead. That also made sense to the banks. Thomke's funding request was approved despite the initial scepticism of the large bank representatives.

Two years before Hayek took over the whole responsibility at the new watch company, the Swatch already had a four-year development path behind it. The activation of a fully automated production line was planned for autumn 1983. From 1985, Hayek became the most important guarantor of the project as the dominant owner of the company. Hayek then strongly nurtured his adoptive child. This is his achievement.

In his book-length interview with the *NZZ* journalist Friedemann Bartu, however, Hayek gives a rather different account of the history of the Swatch's origins. Thomke is portrayed there as a hard-working, technically adept and cost-conscious manager – nothing more and nothing less. Although Thomke was already responsible for all the brands in the lower and middle price segments (such as Swatch, Tissot and Mido) in 1984, Hayek only accords him a very secondary role in the success of the Swatch. For the boss of the Swatch Group today, it is clear to whom most of the credit is due: 'So the first thing I did was take the decision to position the Swatch in the market and I put all my energy into launching it.'

Yet Ernst Thomke had already drawn up the specification in 1979 for this ground-breaking innovation, with which he began to stir up the watch market at the beginning of the 1980s. When, one year earlier, he moved from the research department of the pharmaceutical company Beecham into the watch industry as the new ETA Director-General, he initially only knew this industry from the ground level. Thomke had previously completed watchmaker training at the watch raw-movement manufacturer ETA, after being expelled from his secondary school as a pubescent boy on disciplinary grounds. Because of some problems with an assistant teacher, the headmaster had reproached him for being incapable of accepting discipline. After completing his training, Thomke turned his back on the watch industry in order to take his final school exams at night school. He went on to study medicine. Although it was essential at that time in most Swiss firms to have served as an officer, Thomke remained an ordinary soldier, as the rebel also had his difficulties with authority figures in the army. After his studies he took up a post as a scientific assistant at the British pharmaceutical company Beecham, where he rose to become Marketing Manager for the European division. When the pharmaceutical multinational wanted to send him abroad, Thomke decided on a new direction. As the father of a young family, he had no wish to move away from Switzerland with his school-age children. So he moved to be Director-General of ETA in Grenchen, which he had known well before.

There he was still on first-name terms with half the staff. That was not, of course, enough to prove himself in his new management position. As the most senior person responsible for movements production at ASUAG, Thomke first had to put himself completely in the picture and gather information about the situation in the foreign markets. A journey to the USA provided him with a key experience. One American client, Gerry Grinberg, the head of the American Watch Company, did not have a good word to say in a conversation about the Swiss watch industry. He complained that the watches made in Switzerland were much too thick and too bulky and the marketing in general was also very amateurish. So long mocked as imitators, the Japanese were at that time actually much closer to the market. In New York, Grinberg showed Thomke a thin quartz watch made by the Japanese firm Seiko that was only 2.5 millimetres thick. The watch manager from the dynamic pharmaceutical industry was amazed. Actually Thomke did not need to feel personally affected by this criticism. First, he had only just entered the watch industry and, second, as head of ETA he was only in charge of movements production and not the finished watches. He had to supply the finished watch producers with what they asked for from him. Yet Thomke quickly realised that sooner or later ETA's hopes would be dashed for ever if fewer and fewer Swiss watches were being demanded on the foreign markets. To whom would he go on supplying movements and parts if the Swiss watch industry withdrew further and further into the redoubt of the highest price segment?

Thomke faced a dilemma. In the highly regulated and cartel-dominated industry he was in principle not allowed to concern himself with the finished watches division. Yet the young manager still operated according to the motto 'You don't wait for skills to arrive, you acquire them'. So in summer 1978 he called together the technicians at the Ebauches group for a meeting and described to them the dangerous situation. He set the bar unmistakeably high to his colleagues by saying: 'Within the next six months we want to launch the thinnest watch with the thinnest movement in the world.' A project team immediately set to work.

From this, just a few months later, emerged the Delirium tremens, which in French sounds like 'delirium très mince', that is, very thin delirium. At 1.98 mm thick, it was in fact a wafer-thin watch. With this miniature miracle, the Swiss had defeated the Japanese at least on the technological level. On New Year's Day in 1979, the watch was introduced in New York. It underwent a kind of crash test at the Hudson River because Thomke was completing the marathon run there with a delirium watch on his wrist. For the moment he could be satisfied. The small watch, which was not exactly sporty-looking, still worked perfectly at the end despite the vibrations that it underwent on the 42-kilometre route. Unlike Thomke's average running time, the world record of this thinnest ever watch has yet to be surpassed.

However, the watch was not only thin; it also incorporated a technological innovation. To make it as compact as possible, instead of installing the watch movement in the case, the technicians connected the back of the watch directly with the movement. Removing the need to insert the components into the case brought huge cost savings. This idea was also implemented soon afterwards with the Swatch. Nevertheless, the Delirium is in no sense a precursor of the Swatch, as was constantly rumoured. The Delirium was a gold watch in the upper price segment, the top range – anything but a cheap second or accessory watch like the Swatch. With its retail price of a full 40,000 francs, it could in fact drive an average earner into delirium or madness.

With this watch, the Swiss watch industry had now certainly challenged the Japanese on the technological level. However, this was not enough to halt the retrenchment on the foreign markets and the constant decline in the number of units exported, still less reverse it. That could, in Thomke's view, only be achieved by a cheap watch that could be produced in large quantities with the highest possible automation. At first he saw the solution as the development of a so-called 'Delirium vulgare' – a popular version of the flat luxury watch. Years later, the academic doctor explained to the employees at a Swatch party in medical jargon how they had hit on that terrible name at the time: 'You all know about this dramatically developing illness, this suddenly emerging physiological breakdown that is expressed in delusion.' By this Thomke of course meant the situation of the watch industry at the time, which was in danger of manoeuvring into the delusion of self-sufficiency with its limited way of thinking. In this period of decline, a crazy approach to a solution was required. The breakdown had also been necessary since they had had to break away completely from what had been the usual technologies and jettison all the conventional approaches. With this almost revolutionary concept, no wonder Thomke was considered rather mad by many of the watchmakers who were previously spoilt by success.

Thomke soon saw that a cheap version of the Delirium could not be the solution. On 9 October 1979, he called a few people together again, this time to a brainstorming session at the Chateau de Vaumarcus above Lake Neuenburg. There he outlined the specification for the new kind of watch that he had long had in mind. Thomke was certainly no supporter of the 1968 protesters. But here he seemed to want to adopt the slogan of the student protests of May 1968 in Paris. 'Be realistic – demand the impossible' was chanted in the streets at that time. Thomke's demands actually seemed completely impossible to many participants: this watch was to cost no more than 10 francs. This was a truly ambitious goal given that the production of a watch movement at that time still cost between 25 and 30 francs. The watch also had to be 100 per cent Swiss-made. There was no question of producing it in low-wage countries. It also had to be waterproof, with no after-sales service, as well as having a fully automated assembly. Complete automation was essential if the costs were to be reduced by one third. And a display that showed the hour, minute, second and date was a feature that was taken for granted on a modern watch. The cheap quartz digital watches (with digital display) from Japan would be challenged by an inexpensive electronic Swiss-made watch with an analogue display.

Thomke did not worry too much about how this could possibly be achieved. That was not his problem, but one for the engineers – who just gasped at first. Thomke was confronting them with a completely new perspective for the Swiss watch industry: he was formulating his product requirements for once not from the technician's viewpoint but from the customer's perspective. Until then the engineers had determined what was produced. They specified what the sales department had to provide to customers. For a long time, there was also no reason to change this, since Swiss watches had been in strong demand on the foreign markets for decades.

The cool wind that was now suddenly blowing at ETA began to be felt in Grenchen. The spirit of optimism instigated by Thomke pleased the young plastics expert Elmar Mock and his colleague, who was a few years older, the watch technician Jacques Müller. The 28-year-old Mock was the only plastics engineer at ASUAG at the end of the 1970s.

The two young men had long felt rather understretched at ETA and were now keen to spring into action. A few months after the brainstorming session at the Chateau de Vaumarcus, they attended a technology seminar at Esslingen University in Germany. They were disappointed by the rather dull course. So they spent much of the time talking shop over a beer in various bars. About a dozen new ideas emerged from these relaxed conversations. After their return, Mock and Müller put them down on paper.

Mock's task at ETA was to develop plastic parts for watch movements. This actually meant he was breaking the company's internal rules. Using injection-moulding technology was prohibited at ETA Grenchen at that time because of the division of labour in force. Yet Mock had already received these instructions from Thomke's predecessor, Fritz Scholl. Now he wanted to go one step further, regardless of the company rules. In the many beer-table discussions with Müller in Esslingen, one of the ideas that emerged was in fact to construct a plastic watch on the model of the Delirium in which the movement could also be directly installed into the back. This made it possible to reduce the number of parts in the watch by around two thirds. Yet the two engineers lacked the necessary machinery to build the prototype for such a watch. Although ETA was actually not permitted to operate in the finished watch sector, they had the bold idea of asking the head office for a loan for an injection-moulding machine. The most suitable models for their purposes were not cheap. At the firm Netstal in the canton of Glarus, one of these high-tech machines cost around 250,000 francs. In a crisis period, in which one round of cost-cutting was closely followed by another, that was an enormous sum.

When the young engineers' capital expenditure request reached Thomke's desk, he had them summoned by his secretary at eleven o'clock on 27 March 1980 to a one o'clock meeting in his office. After a short, dry greeting Thomke gave them a telling-off. With their unauthorised actions, the two boffins had bypassed the official channels. Yet when Mock and Müller presented the drawings for their project, Thomke shot up from his chair as if electrified: 'That's exactly what I'm after!' Thomke approved the funding on the spot without informing anyone. In order not to cause a fuss, the funding was divided into several tranches and the machine was ordered from Netstal in individual parts by stages. The board of directors at the Ebauches group was only informed in early 1981.

Then a conspiratorial team set to work. The meeting invitations did not include members of the ASUAG management board. Even the invitation to the meeting that took place on 16 April 1981 at the Stierenberg restaurant in the Grenchen mountains did not feature any of the top bosses. What Thomke still lacked was a marketing expert. He looked for someone who was untainted by the prevailing company culture and did not come from the watch industry. He remembered Franz Xaver Sprecher, an acquaintance from his time at Beecham. Sprecher was then working for the firm Jäggi Communications in

Bern, which was later sold to Burson-Marsteller, on the same floor
as Thomke. Sprecher knew nothing about the watch business, but
he had a great deal of experience in fashion and consumer goods
marketing and so he fitted the job profile exactly. Thomke hired him
for a brainstorming session in Stierenberg and the fee came to 500
francs. The key members of Thomke's team were Jacques Müller and
Elmar Mock for the construction, Walter Salathé for the production
and Franz Xaver Sprecher for the marketing. For the injection-
moulding technology side, experts were also brought in from the toy
manufacturer Lego.

Shortly after the Stierenberg meeting, Thomke invited Sprecher to his
house above Grenchen on the Jura arc to exchange ideas. The former
rectory had just been renovated. On the top floor, the two traced the
developmental stages of the new watch in chalk on the roughcast of
the brick walls. It would still probably be possible to scratch down to
the sketches under the roughcast today. Since the appeal of the new in
such consumer items always quickly fades, Thomke and Sprecher took
the view that the success of this new product was only guaranteed in
the long run if fashionable new models could be created continually.
This watch could not be allowed to be a one-hit wonder. Sprecher
consequently took on the commission for executing and transforming
the marketing concept for the new watch as a freelance project.

In parallel, the engineers at ETA worked flat-out to develop
prototypes. Thomke granted the team great freedom and consciously
allowed a form of controlled chaos. As an opponent of over-regimented
procedures himself, he realised that a creative process required some
freedom to mess around. Mock recalls: 'At the same time, though,
Thomke was also highly demanding. He put our team under immense
pressure to succeed.' Unless one person takes decisions and assumes
responsibility in such projects, they are doomed to fail from the outset.
But Thomke never thought much of collective decisions anyway. Among
his critics, he therefore has a Machiavellian reputation. But Thomke
always took this as a compliment rather than an insult.

Just before Christmas 1981, the prototypes of the new watch
became available. It was a truly difficult birth. New problems kept
arising. At the beginning, the hands even ran backwards. There was
one breakdown after another, and yet finally the moment came. The
ETA staff were gathered together at the Christmas party and some of

the employees were already saying goodbye and wishing each other happy holidays. Mock and Müller, who had been working up to the last minute on their new development in the workshop, brought five prototypes, all nicely arranged on a cushion, into Thomke's office. For Thomke, that was the best possible Christmas present.

His happiness was short-lived though. A few days after Christmas, Sprecher called from his skiing holiday in Zermatt to tell him that one of the test watches he had taken had stood still on the descent from Gornergrat. Thomke called his two young employees back into his office before the New Year. While all the rest of the ETA staff could enjoy their holidays, Mock and Müller had to solve the problem that had just emerged. After a long test phase, they finally succeeded and the prototypes finally worked perfectly. For ETA this was almost a historic moment, for this development later enabled the company to register a total of seven patents. For Mock and Müller, though, the great effort was not very well remunerated. They each received a bonus of 700 francs for an invention that in the following years made billions in revenue. But with this measly payment, the two boffins were in good company in Swiss business history. The inventor of the sedative Valium, a medicine that developed into a genuine bestseller, received just one dollar in payment at the end of the 1950s.

The first systematic tests were then carried out on its accuracy and its resistance to knocks and other strains. The new watch still had no name. The marketing expert Sprecher collected on a sheet of paper around five dozen partly very bizarre ideas, from Just-a-watch to Funwatch. To these were added some suggestions he received from the American advertising agency McCann Erickson in New York. The American advertisers advised him to create an association in the buyer's mind with the Swiss-made origin designation, with names such as 'Swisswatch', 'Second watch', 'S'Watches' or 'Swiss Watch'. On the return flight from the USA, Sprecher distilled from a shortlist of these ideas the name 'Swatch'. He simply began to strike out the letters between the 'S' standing for 'Switzerland' and the English word 'Watch' until he was left with the word 'Swatch'.

In summer 1982, the city of Dallas in the USA was chosen as a test market. The launch turned into a flop, though, because there was no coherent marketing concept. Also, the 10,000 manually assembled Swatch watches looked rather conservative. The advertising budget was far too small. Marvin Traub, then CEO of Bloomingdales department store, immediately gave Thomke a lesson in consumer goods marketing: 'You can only turn your watch into a fashion product if you throw half a dozen new collections onto the market every year. Otherwise you'll never succeed!' Such an intensive market cultivation was new even to Thomke.

Until then, Thomke had seen the Swatch primarily as a weapon in the battle against the Japanese competition rather than as a new lifestyle product. Under pressure from the aggressive Japanese competition, the Swatch team actually thought in military terms. The language was also correspondingly martial. One of the papers circulating at ETA featured the phrase 'Kill the Japs'. An ugly military green was used for the first Swatch models, as if it were a watch manufactured in an army contract. They still lacked a creative industrial designer to generate ideas. Only when this person was found did they have the courage to give the dials and straps a colourful and imaginative form.

After the consultation with a well-known design team in Zurich, the cheap watch was finally turned into a fashionable second accessory watch. There were still almost no accessory watches up to this point in time. With traditional watches that consisted of up to 150 parts, the manufacturing period was far too long for that. There was not enough adaptability to respond immediately to fashion trends. The Swatch, though, now consisting of only around 50 parts with its plastic case, opened up the possibility of constantly changing the appearance of the watch. Now up to four new collections were launched every year. As a second watch, the Swatch was intended for people who normally wore an expensive watch like a Rolex or a Patek Philippe but wanted to leave it at home when they went skiing or jogging. With regard to this market segment, the Swatch could not therefore be promoted as a cheap watch in any way.

The Swatch team now concentrated fully on building the brand. At the beginning there were still some critics and sceptics. For instance, the watch was criticised for ticking too loud and not being repairable. There, too, the Swatch team managed to find a solution: the weaknesses were simply converted into strengths. Certainly, the Swatch engineers tried to reduce slightly the volume of the ticking. Because the 'tick-tock' could not be completely eliminated, however, they made a virtue of the necessity: 'A Swatch has to tick; only then is it alive', was the message.

And in the USA the slogan was short and snappy: 'Fashion that ticks'. To the objection that the watch was not repairable, Thomke and his people also had a ready answer: a watch repair usually costs much more than a new Swatch. Besides, the Swatch was of such high quality that it would never have to be repaired.

Nevertheless, there were some teething troubles in the market launch. For two pins, Thomke would have entrusted the distribution of this new development in the USA to the major client Timex. Yet the firm showed little interest. He also spoke to Migros. The Migros head, Arnold, invited Thomke to Zurich at the headquarters of the Migros cooperative association, to smoked salmon sandwiches and a glass of champagne. Yet Arnold wanted to launch the watch as its own brand according to the Migros philosophy. That, however, was not what the Swatch inventor had in mind. As a traditional movements producer that had mutated into a finished watches manufacturer, ETA did not want to enter into a new dependency with this watch. Thomke declined. When Arnold learnt of the refusal, he immediately launched a similar product on the market with the help of the Zurich Mondaine Watch. Migros even managed to launch this M-watch a few months before the Swatch. Like almost all the raw movements in Swiss watches, that of the Migros watch also came from ETA in Grenchen. Nevertheless, this did not generate any serious competition for Swatch. It is a historical irony that shortly after the launch of the M-watch Arnold took over the presidency of the SMH group at Hayek's request and thus also the highest responsibility for the Swatch.

Now Thomke's search for partners was over. He decided to launch the Swatch under his own management. On 1 March 1983 he presented the new watch to the Swiss media. And in autumn that same year a new start was made in the USA, one year after the bellyflop on this market. No half-measures were taken this time with the advertising, and the launch was rewarded with a real bestseller. The communication and promotion budget was almost as big as the production budget. This even outstripped the cosmetics industry, which until then had always put the largest sums into cultivating their markets. In America, a real cult of the Swatch soon arose. The main person responsible for the success was Max Imgrüth, from Lucerne, who soon acquired the nickname Mad Max. The bustling marketing man caused a sensation partly because he had his photo taken for a poster in the leather gear of the film hero of that name. Imgrüth, who came from the textile industry, ensured that the Swatch was not simply perceived as a conventional watch this time, but as a lifestyle product. He himself always wore a Swatch on each wrist. When he was asked why he was wearing two watches, he replied: 'Because I've forgotten the third one'. Imgrüth achieved the feat of raising the turnover within two years from $1 million to $75 million.

Thomke realised that almost everything that comes from the USA sooner or later succeeds in Europe and in Switzerland too. He therefore drew much of his inspiration from the experience he gained in the American market. 'The Swatch must always remain up-to-date and be different from the rest', he demanded. The Swatch also brought a revolution in distribution. From the outset, the watch was passed directly to the retailer, cutting out the middleman. This policy prevented any of the margin being creamed off by third parties.

Discount stores and kiosks had no place in this concept. High-quality department stores, boutiques and fashion houses were chosen as sales outlets in addition to the specialist watch shops. This restrictive distribution policy was critical to its success. Because it was not being sold like any ordinary cheap watch, the Swatch also gained the confidence of the specialist shops established in the high price segment. They gained the opportunity to set up a separate Swatch corner next to their expensive prestige brands. This meant the jazziness and trendiness of the watch could be emphasised. Hayek later went one step further by opening a series of Swatch stores, including at the smartest addresses such as the Place Vendôme in Paris, with its group of luxury shops around the Ritz hotel.

In Switzerland, though, there were many watch dealers who did not at first understand this concept. They believed that a plastic watch costing only 50 francs had no place alongside a Patek Philippe or a Rolex. The snobbery of some specialist dealers went even further at the beginning. When Thomke's close friend Franz Sprecher indicated early in 1983 at the Basel watch fair, where the cream of the industry gathers every year, that he was there as the Swatch representative, he was even thrown out of the 'Temple of the Pharisees' as a 'traitor'.

Yet the massive sales figures in time gave even the sceptics pause for thought. Whereas in November 1982 only a few hundred swatches were produced, by 1985 there were one million every month. In the first five years, 268 different models were created and 50 million watches were sold. ETA, which had also been torn apart in the vortex of the watch crisis as a parts supplier, managed to pull itself up by its bootstraps like Munchhausen himself with the finished Swatch product.

In time, the Swatch production costs could even be cut to below the initial target level of 10 francs. With the classic simple Swatch, it was only 5 francs. With a standard retail price of 50 francs, this produced a handsome margin. Now even the Japanese companies Seiko and Hattori sought out Thomke. They wanted to learn at first hand how this success was possible.

An essential contribution to this was made not least by Jacques Irniger, who arrived at Swatch in autumn 1983. He brought his experiences from the consumer goods marketing of Nestlé, Colgate and other world-famous brands. In a relatively short time, the Swatch became a global brand. The watch became a cult on the European markets as well. To underline its fun quality, they had the idea of hanging a 13.5-ton, 165-metre-long mega-Swatch on the building of the Deutsche Commerzbank in Frankfurt. This giant watch gained an entry in the *Guinness Book of Records*. By this campaign, the marketing people wanted to emphasise that there was no gulf between the very cheap watch and the wealthy customers of this bank. More of these mega-watches hung in the following years in Barcelona and Tokyo, among other places. And abroad the much smaller maxi-Swatch, still two metres long, was soon part of the interior fittings of every Swiss embassy. One of these still hangs in the kitchen at Thomke's house in Grenchen.

To make an emotional impact on consumers, ambassadors were sought for the Swatch. In France, the film actress Catherine Deneuve was acquired as a Swatch representative. The film actor Jack Nicholson also had his photo taken with Swatch watches. The artist Andy Warhol also collected the plastic objects by the dozen. From 1984, the Swatch boom made an essential contribution to an upward trend across the whole Swiss watch industry. The innovation not only gave fresh impetus to the whole industry but also restored some of its self-confidence. At this time the Swatch and the scratchproof Rado, with its traditionally strong base in the Middle East, were the only profit-making company brands.

Federal Councillor Kurt Furgler receives the 10-millionth Swatch in 1985,
accompanied by Pierre Arnold, President of the SMH board of directors, and
Nicolas Hayek. © Keystone.

In autumn 1985 when Nicolas Hayek took over the majority
shareholding of the watch company with a group of investors, 10
million Swatch watches had already been produced and sold. Shortly
after he had concluded the pool agreement with his investors group,
Hayek was able formally to present the 10-millionth Swatch to Federal
Councillor Kurt Furgler.

However, the Swatch very narrowly avoided becoming a victim of its
own phenomenal success. The rising demand began to result in supply
shortages. They wanted to avoid as far as possible incurring costs by
building up warehouse stocks. Yet even in this critical situation, the
Swatch team managed to make the best of it. For they very quickly
realised that the harder the Swatch was to obtain, the more people
wanted it. The Swatch people then began to launch limited editions
and made the watch a collectable item. In 1986 the first watch auction
took place at Sotheby's in Geneva. ETA produced collectors' albums
for it. At Christie's auction house, the price for individual models very
quickly rose to 20,000 francs. The collecting frenzy continued until
1996 at the Atlanta Olympics, after which it clearly waned.

Year by year, Hayek's SMH sold more Swatch watches. In 1992 the production figure passed the 100 million mark. The plastic watch had already produced a turnover of over half a billion francs. Nicolas Hayek arranged to celebrate this record with a grand party in Zermatt. On this occasion a Sonore Swatch was also presented. The wearer of this alarm-watch could wake up to the French pop star Jean-Michel Jarre's music. Jarre composed for the promotional occasion at the Walliser ski resort a fantastic light, laser and music show in tribute. Some Zermatt residents had to switch off their lights at home so that everyone could get the full benefit of the spectacle. The party cost around 10 million francs. Hayek chose the location because 'with the million-year-old Matterhorn it symbolises Swiss and European naturalness and originality and stands for everything I have advocated all my life. Also it doesn't smell of car fumes like other famous spa resorts.' Hayek invited 1,200 guests to the party, including the Federal Councillors Flavio Cotti and Jean-Pascal Delamuraz, the former Federal Councillor Nello Celio, the entrepreneur Stephan Schmidheiny, and 450 journalists

Nicolas Hayek with his wife Marianne (left) and Federal Councillor Jean-Pascal Delamuraz at the Zermatt celebration party in 1992 for the first 100 million Swatches produced.

from all over the world. The American television broadcaster NBC and
the British BBC were also there. At the press conference at the trendy
bar Vernissage, journalists were even applauding the watch king. That
is highly unusual for people in the media who are concerned for their
independence because it is regarded as ingratiating.

Hayek had his guests greeted in a marquee by TV presenter Kurt
Aeschbacher. Kirchgasse, which runs alongside the graveyard in which
almost every other gravestone is a memorial to a mountain walker
who met his death, was renamed 'Swatch Twin Phone Street'. Hayek
could hardly take a step without being thronged by people wanting his
autograph. 'He beamed with happiness like a little child', remembers
one of the guests who stood next to him. It was only after the official
guests had left that the real celebrations began for the Swatch fans
and collectors. Around 60,000 people streamed into the Walliser
mountain village over the weekend. One fan who had travelled from
Duisburg queued for a total of 15 hours at the sales kiosks until he had
picked up the seven more Swatch watches that he was missing. For the
anniversary, a special 'Swatch the people' watch was sold there for the
first time. Nevertheless, the massive advertising spectacle was not only
a Swatch party but much more also a celebration in Hayek's honour.
Not only Federal Councillor Delamuraz, but also the Director of the
Rio Summit, Maurice Strong, congratulated the watch industrialist on
his success in a welcoming speech.

No one said another word about Thomke's or Mock's achievements
in developing this watch. Thomke had parted company with Hayek
one year earlier and Mock had left the company six years previously.
Neither was invited to the celebration – a bitter disappointment for
them both. Even in Hayek's inner circle many heads were shaken at
this petty-mindedness. Yet it could do nothing to dent the celebratory
mood. Hayek instead used the occasion to present himself as the Father
of the Swatch. He presented a book that, as he put it, told 'the true
story for the first time' about the invention of the Swatch. It claims to
'refute the myths circulating about how the Swatch came about'. Long
before Thomke arrived at ETA, the head of Ebauches Fontainemelon,
André Beyer, had had the idea of building a cheaper watch on the
same principle as the Delirium. He, Hayek, had then decided to launch
the Swatch based on this idea. This version has become the official
historical narrative of the Swatch Group. It has since been taken up by

a broad section of the media. This is despite the fact that this account directly contradicts all the published statements of the Swatch press office in the 1980s.

People have waited in vain to this day for Thomke's version of how the Swatch came into existence. In the few interviews he has given since then, he has always refused to comment on his quarrel with Hayek. Thomke is very reluctant to talk about this episode in his managerial career, as an episode that is riddled with disappointments. However, he certainly does not see himself as anything like the 'father' or even the 'inventor' of the Swatch. 'All the brilliant ideas that gave rise to the Swatch came from our engineers and marketing people. I was only the catalyst that pointed the way', is how he now describes his role then. As a non-technician, he had merely drawn up the specification from the consumer perspective. However, Mock, who came up with a large part of the technical concept, corrects this slightly: 'Without Thomke, the Swatch would never have happened.' Mock's disappointment is also still palpable today. After he left the watch group, he set up his own company. Three years later, over a curry scampi he had ordered from Mövenpick at the Hayek Engineering offices, Hayek had tried to bring him back. Although things had been going very badly at his firm, which specialised in developing products and concepts, Mock had refused. Meanwhile, his Creaholic firm in Biel, working with companies such as Tetra Pak, Nestlé, Roche and Boehringer Ingelheim Pharma, has grown into a flourishing creative consultancy with around 30 employees. His colleague Jacques Müller is the only member of that team still working at the Swatch Group today. Some Swatch people later lost their lives in an aeroplane accident in Göppingen when the hired single-engine Piper Aztec plunged into thick fog.

However, what carries more weight than the views of these two people who were directly involved, whose wounds are obviously still raw, is Jochem Thieme's account. Hayek's closest colleague in the watch industry at that time summarises his account as follows:

> The development of the Swatch goes back to 1978 – long before we at Hayek Engineering had started our work in the watch industry. Purely on that basis Nick Hayek [he means Nicolas G.] certainly cannot be the 'Father of the Swatch', as is often wrongly claimed. Nick Hayek has achieved such great things in his life that there is no need to give him credit for things that were not his own doing.

However, Thieme considers that Thomke's role in the launch of the Swatch is totally underestimated today.

It is a fact that the plastic watch already accounted for three quarters of the finished watch sales of the ASUAG/SSIH group in volume terms when Hayek took over at SMH. With its sales proceeds, the watch then surpassed not only the Longines brand but also Rado. It was, however, Hayek's financial and business involvement that first made possible the long-term success of this plastic quartz watch and thus the recovery of the Swiss watch industry. It was his achievement to have made the Swatch Group the global leader in the watch industry. By launching the Swatch, Thomke laid the foundations for this achievement.

6

The Thin Air on the Way to the Top – how the Successful Hayek and Thomke Duo Came to an End

TWO MONTHS AFTER THE investors' consortium took over the majority stake, Hayek publicised the new proprietors' plans. The first press conference took place in the Hotel Elite in Biel rather than in Zurich, as is usual for large firms. By this Hayek wanted to demonstrate his affinity with the watchmaking region. Unlike almost all companies quoted on the stock exchange, he never proceeded to hold his press conferences in the financial capital. As well as Hayek, Pierre Arnold as President of the board of directors and Ernst Thomke as the head of the watch division gave some explanations to the press.

Hayek, Arnold and Thomke were able for the first time to report a striking improvement in the group's turnover and revenue. By launching the Swatch, the merged watch group had already taken the first important step on the path to success. As well as the Swatch, the Rado, well-established in the Middle East, also developed positively. Unlike the other brands, this watch, which very early had caused a stir with a scratchproof alloy case, had never gone into the red. The rising number of Swatch units contributed to a strong improvement in the production capacity for the parts and raw movements at ETA.

The triumvirate presented a series of measures for strengthening the group's profitability. Hayek had one main wish: to gain more freedom of manoeuvre and get the banks out of the company as fast as possible. To do so, he had to reduce some large debts. He had already hinted at his suspicion of the financial institutions. 'The bankers are great financial experts but they don't know much about industry', he is still convinced today. He had great confidence only in Peter Gross, Director-General of the Union Bank, for it was he who had persuaded the banks to follow Hayek's advice and not allow ASUAG and SSIH to fail. The nearly 80-year-old Gross still sits on the board of directors of the Swatch Group today – no longer, of course, as a bank representative but in a personal capacity.

Once the newly formed watch group was on the right track to creating a solid industrial base in the lowest price segment, it was time to take a second step in order to get Omega back on course. It was Hayek's goal to challenge the global brand Rolex again as soon as possible. The strongest competitor had never got into difficulties, whereas at Omega this was already the third reorganisation attempt. In the boardroom corridors at Jakob-Stämpfli Straße in Biel, a stream of around a dozen Director-Generals had come and gone over the previous ten years. None of them had succeeded in clearly positioning the brand and achieving a turnaround. They just continued to muddle along. The product catalogues contained the baffling figure of around 800 models in around 1,500 different versions. The multiplicity of models sprouting ever more grotesque blooms sent the production costs soaring; the batches were far too small to be manufactured cost-effectively. There were Omega watches in almost every price bracket, and the expensive versions even included some with gold-plated internal parts. Consumers had little use for gimmicks of this kind. The more models were created, the more difficult it became for the consumer to see the wood for the trees. No one knew what this brand stood for any longer. With its name taken from the last letter of the Greek alphabet, which stands metaphorically for 'completion', Omega was literally in danger of approaching its own end. However, only Thomke and Hayek had dared to speak this truth out loud till now.

The previous management teams had always tried to hush up the decline of the prestige brand. So the parent company in Biel had forced the foreign subsidiaries in the USA, Italy and France to take on excessive quantities of the increasingly expensive finished watches. By recording a fat margin, the Biel staff were certainly able to stabilise their francs revenue with this ruse and create the impression that the Omega watches were still in demand. Yet this tactic over the years led to losses in the region of tens of millions of francs. Only insiders knew that the brand was increasingly losing its appeal to consumers. No business report ever mentioned that the warehouses in the foreign subsidiaries were overflowing with unsaleable watches.

'Once a reputation is ruined, it lives on totally unrestrained', goes the popular saying. This was not entirely true of Omega, though. The management certainly behaved without restraint. The reputation of the brand was, however, amazingly not at all ruined on the global markets; on the contrary, Omega remained the most famous international watch brand apart from Rolex. Hayek had quickly seen the potential that lay in this evocative name. He asked Thomke to make a new start and to make Omega a beacon of the Swiss watch industry once again. Thomke agreed to this on one condition: that Peter Gross should not have any further say in Omega, for the banker was always interfering in the model policy. Thomke and Gross were therefore never to have a pleasant conversation.

Hayek agreed and gave Thomke a free hand. The academic doctor got straight down to work and prescribed a painful, drastic cure for Omega. He slashed the number of staff to one third of the previous headcount. At the same time he increased it by taking on more than two dozen marketing experts. They were all specialists with no previous experience of the watch industry. For Thomke, that was in fact an important condition for their appointment. He wanted only people who were untainted by the stench of the pre-existing culture in the industry. Thomke radically tightened up the product range by reducing the number of models to one sixth. The treatment worked wonders. The next year Omega went back into the black after a long period. Productivity steadily increased. In the following years the added value gradually rose from 70,000 to 165,000 francs per employee.

At Longines, too, everything was dismantled. This slightly cheaper brand is just behind Omega in the price hierarchy. Overlaps were eliminated and entire sections of the manufacturing were phased out and allocated to ETA, which had emerged from Ebauches SA. Hayek gave the restructuring task to the Marketing Director, Walter von Känel. He had joined Longines in 1969 and was therefore strongly rooted in this brand's traditional company culture. However, to Hayek's annoyance von Känel acted rather obstructively at the beginning. The local hero who had grown up in St Immer, where the company was based, tended to prioritise the preservation of existing jobs over his instructions. At the time von Känel was the only senior executive of the group who dared to contradict Hayek openly. 'Le père Hayek', as he still likes to call his boss today in his absence, therefore punished him from time to time by removing responsibilities. It is not that Hayek would brook no contradiction from his employees. But it was worth sticking to certain rules when dealing with him. 'In private you can use plain language with him', says Hans-Jürg Schär, former head of Swatch and later the Micro Car Company. When other people are listening, however, Hayek seriously dislikes being contradicted.

Von Känel also had to learn this over time. Ultimately he could not avoid cutting 150 jobs at Longines in accordance with the instructions from the group management. By obeying his most senior boss, he smoothed the way for being brought into the expanded group management very quickly. Von Känel is now the only person left from the old ASUAG management team. He was in fact a 'faithful soldier', as the regiment commander used to say. Even in his activities outside work, he complied with his boss's wishes. Von Känel would have liked to become a brigadier as a successor to François Habersaat, then Director of the Fédération Horlogère. Yet Hayek had prevented him, according to people in the industry. Unlike most other Swiss industrial firms, there were hardly any senior officers at management level in the watch industry. Hayek also managed to talk von Känel out of becoming a candidate on the list of Liberal National Councillors. To lick the newly formed company into shape, he needed all hands on deck.

In Thomke, however, Hayek had a man at the most senior management level who could not be so easily tamed. Because of the way their work was divided, the two of them made an unbeatable winning team at first. Hayek secured the financing of the company and set the course as the visionary thinker and strategist. And Thomke implemented it. As a prominent figurehead, Pierre Arnold, President of the board of directors, was given the role of ensuring public goodwill. At that time Hayek did not yet have the authority and reputation that he does today. However, Arnold did not have any great influence in the watch group. The former Migros boss concluded his career with this appointment.

At first Hayek still based his work at his consultancy firm in Zurich, while Thomke stayed in his former office at ETA in Grenchen. Because of the spatial distance, the two alpha-leaders could not get in each other's way. Yet the potential for a major conflict was already there, as Hayek and Thomke were differently wired.

Almost everyone who ever worked with these two strong personalities said that their two characters were simply incompatible. Neither liked any interference. Their philosophies of life were fundamentally different. Thomke loved launching new projects as a mentor and directing employees in its implementation. Once it was all working fine, things soon got too dull for him. Then he would seek out a new area of activity. So Thomke did not shrink from simultaneously tackling the reorganisation of the technology firm Saurer and acting as a troubleshooter for Bally, the specialist consumer goods firm. As he likes to operate in several places at the same time, he was also already being criticised for spreading himself too thinly with his commitments. Unlike Hayek, Thomke takes personal criticism very calmly. Prestige and recognition seem to leave him cold. Although he is already entering his eighth decade, today Thomke is still involved in instigating and financing a whole series of smaller companies. These are mainly projects that do not bring him great acclaim or particularly large sums of money. Thomke is satisfied if he is respected by people who are important to him.

Hayek, however, worked extremely single-mindedly to build his entrepreneurial career from the outset. This determination is said to be evident in everything that he does. There is always a firm purpose behind his actions, according to people who have worked closely with him. Unlike Thomke, Hayek acquired a very large amount of capital relatively early. That enabled him to get into the watch industry as a leading investor. Hayek has a sound instinct for good opportunities. Like Thomke, most of his energy certainly comes from his inner motivation, but Hayek is also driven by another source of energy: as well as his enjoyment of work, he has a strong appetite for recognition. The Lebanese immigrant who was initially ostracised by the Swiss business establishment wanted to prove them all wrong. As the saviour of the watch industry he has since undoubtedly succeeded there. No one, even Thomke, will be able to dispute this.

However differently these two business leaders may operate, they also have a few important points in common, which have played a key part in their entrepreneurial success. In a presentation to the Swiss Management Association (ASOS), Thomke once listed the qualities that make a true entrepreneur:

> innovators often have an unusual personality structure and are rare creatures. Besides intelligence, which other people also have, they show intellectual flexibility, strong communication skills, willingness to take risks, charisma, capacity to carry things through at all levels, willingness to learn,

capacity for enthusiasm about something new, and an ability to break away from convention.

These characteristics apply to both Hayek and Thomke. They are both distinctly combative characters. When he still played tennis regularly, Hayek made an all-out effort on court as if his personal honour were also slightly at stake. Once when he competed with the tennis star Martina Hingis in front of over 100 invited journalists, he put all his effort into the game. It did not particularly bother him that the outcome of the match was a foregone conclusion. For him the main point was to present the number one in ladies' tennis as an ambassador for Omega.

Hayek and Thomke also have some key traits in common that, when combined at the highest management level of a company, easily become a spanner in the works and poison the working atmosphere. They are distinctly egocentric and react in a highly emotional and impulsive way when something does not go their way. They both tend to polarise people. As bosses, either they are loved and admired by their employees or they are hated. Both Hayck and Thomke show few inhibitions about attacking their opponents in front of an audience if something does not suit them. In the case of Ernst Thomke, I have already experienced that myself. Thomke reprimanded me at a press conference in 1981 at Ebauches Electronic SA in Marin in front of a few dozen colleagues because, as editor of the daily newspaper *Der Bund*, I had not correctly reproduced his so-called ice-hockey stick theory. So that I should finally understand it, Thomke scribbled his curve on the flipchart. With a downward zigzagging line he tried to portray the causal connection between price rises and the drop in sales that inevitably follows. He wanted to demonstrate that consumers always immediately react negatively to price rises. Sales drop again just after a price-determined upward movement, which, graphically portrayed, looks like an ice-hockey stick. Thomke was greatly concerned that everyone should understand his theorem. He was actually the only person at the ASUAG Group at the time who dared openly to lambast the failed pricing policy of his fellow managers. He was therefore feared not only by his subordinates but also by his colleagues. Even his colleague Elmar Mock, the co-inventor of Swatch, still had a healthy respect for his boss. Even when he no longer worked under him, he still found it difficult for a long time to reply to Thomke with the informal 'you' that he used with him.

Hayek, too, can put his opponent straight extremely bluntly when he does not feel understood. When the *Rundschau* presenter Hannes Britschgi, in an interview in 1997, ventured to put some perspective on the scale of the Swatch Group's environmental commitment, Hayek tried to show him up as an idiot in front of a few hundred thousand television viewers. This was despite the fact that Britschgi had previously also taken great trouble to enumerate Hayek's eco-political achievements. He nevertheless felt attacked and reacted in a highly irritated way: 'Don't interrupt me, young man', he said and got down from the red *Rundschau* chair. It would probably only have taken one more provocative remark from Britschgi for Hayek to have left the studio in protest. After that he hardly allowed the television presenter to finish asking a question.

Yet apart from these occasional angry outbursts at unacceptable interview questions, Hayek has an extraordinary talent for communication. When he feels that his partner in conversation is well-disposed towards him, he knows masterfully how to win him over. He can then almost give someone the feeling that they are an immensely important person to him. What journalist does not feel flattered when Hayek tells him he is one of the few in his profession who understands anything about the watch industry? Hayek has a very keen sense of whether people have a favourable attitude to him. For him, though, there seems to be only black and white, friend or foe. Anyone who leaves the Swatch Group often becomes a *persona non grata* for the watch boss, according to several former executives.

Nevertheless, hardly any of these 'renegades' would wish to have missed the time they spent working for Hayek. Everywhere people say they have learnt a great deal at the Swatch Group. Anyone who has worked at this company has extremely good prospects of an interesting, well-paid job. Since the company acts as a springboard for many marketing people, supervisors and other specialist staff, there has always been a very high turnover. 'If you stay too long at the Swatch Group, you're in danger of burning out there', explains one former supervisor. He said he was squeezed out like an orange. There were times when the marketing people at Swatch changed almost every month. But some of these people had to leave the job because they thought they knew it all better and could give Hayek a lesson in marketing.

Despite the many changes, there is still a large number of executive employees today from the earliest days in the inner group management. These include the company lawyer Hanspeter Rentsch, Finance Director Edgar Geiser and Rado boss Roland Streule. These key figures around Hayek and his son were later joined by Arlette Emch. Nicolas Hayek had always had a soft spot for the academic ethnologist who used to work in communications. He nurtured her strongly, not entirely to the pleasure of the other members of the management team. Hayek junior and his sister Nayla were at loggerheads with Emch, according to some insiders. In the inner group management, Emch is responsible for Léon Hatot, Calvin Klein watches and jewellery and for all the jewellery lines together, as well as the Swatch brand. Hayek had introduced a matrix organisation in the mid 1990s by creating an expanded group management of 17 members. Each member of the group management has since been responsible for an individual country in addition to his assigned brand. Hayek has thereby counteracted the parochial mindset of the brand manager and simultaneously achieved a flattening of the hierarchy. He has also in this way secured some influence on all three levels of the hierarchy.

These long-serving group management members have all understood how to adapt to Hayek's patriarchal leadership style. Hayek is revered by them like a father. This submission ranges from natural respect to sometimes almost servile behaviour. How far this subordination can occasionally go is illustrated by an anecdote told by a former supervisor about one of the weekly budget meetings. Hayek is said to have dropped a pencil on the floor in the middle of a discussion. Immediately the group management member Edgar Geiser disappeared in a flash under the table in his suit and tie and searched around wildly on all fours for Hayek's pencil. But in return for the deference that is accorded to him, the watch magnate also gives something back to his closest colleagues. Anyone who stays firmly bound in heart and soul to the company will hardly ever be left in the lurch by him.

Thomke lacks this paternalistic and patriarchal trait. He has constantly brought in other work teams, and often made the wrong choice of employee and partner. This old soldier lacks Hayek's almost feminine intuition. More than once he has been outmanoeuvred by his clients in contracts to reorganise industrial firms. More often these efforts ended in a big disappointment, for example at Bally. 'I had enough of being managed by people who did not keep the promises made when I was appointed and who also had absolutely no expertise', was how, in 1998, he explained his departure from the shoe manufacturer in the *SonntagsZeitung*. As at Hayek's SMH, he also became almost the master–knave at the Bührle subsidiary Bally. At Bührle too, there was a strong minority shareholder who ran the business as if it belonged to him alone. So Thomke also threw in the towel very soon here, because the corrosive conflicts spoilt it for him.

Nicolas Hayek as party host at his daughter Nayla's stud farm in 1987; on the right, Pierre Arnold, President and delegate of the SMH board of directors. © Keystone.

What received most public attention, however, was Thomke's departure from Hayek's SMH. Before the situation developed into an open rift, outsiders still long believed that harmony reigned on the boss's floor of the watch group. In Thomke's circle it was known that he hoped one day to be appointed CEO by Hayek. For Thomke had successfully managed all the group's watch brands since 1985. But Hayek had other plans. Thomke was extremely frustrated when he realised that he had cherished vain hopes, according to people who

observed him closely at the time. At Hayek's 60th birthday party at his
daughter Nayla's stud farm, everyone certainly behaved as if it was all
sweetness and light. Thomke played along in honour of his boss and
did not allow anything to be noticed.

Until this point in time Thomke had still enjoyed relatively large
freedom of manoeuvre in the company. Hayek concentrated on his work
at Hayek Engineering and very rarely came to Biel. Usually Thomke
travelled to Zurich to give his boss a progress report on the business.
However, Hayek began to pester him almost day and night with phone
calls and kept assigning him new tasks. Thomke was getting closer
and closer to the limit of what he could achieve. At least, though, the
geographical distance enabled him to get away from Hayek's control to
some extent. Then from summer 1988 the SMH boss began to take a
tighter grip on the reins. It was shortly after Hayek's 60th birthday – a
time when most businessmen gradually begin to withdraw from their
business – that Hayek now moved the focus of his activity from Zurich
to Biel. Almost every day now he drove his old silver-grey Mercedes CL
Coupé from Meisterschwanden in Aargau to the group headquarters.

Nicolas Hayek and Ernst Thomke in 1989. © Keystone.

The 97 kilometres that he still travels today in the early morning and
late in the evening, partly on the very busy A1, were never an obstacle
for him. As he tells everyone who finds it strange, the car is his thinking
space in which he mulls over ideas along to Mozart and develops his

plans. Hayek uses his time in the car very intensively. He owned one of the first mobile phones. For a few early risers among the journalists who knew his number, he was already contactable before the offices opened. Just before he drove back home, he would make phone calls all round the globe. For his discussion partners in Asia that was no problem, and those in the USA just had to get used to being woken up in the night. Up to eight o'clock in the morning Hayek knew what all his direct subordinates were doing. Any senior executive who had not yet received a call at this time had to interpret this as a bad sign. It was often the signal that the person concerned had lost status or even fallen out of favour.

In the Seevorstadt building in Biel, Hayek moved into the large corner office on the upper management floor that his predecessors had occupied in the former ASUAG company. The strictly hierarchically minded watch barons then still clearly kept their employees at a distance. This was in complete contrast to Hayek – unlike the ASUAG Director-General Peter Renggli, the red light on his door indicating he was not to be disturbed was very rarely on. Just as Hayek expects his employees to be available at any time, he, too, is almost always accessible to them. He is an approachable boss.

Now that he was mainly working in Biel, he tried to take Thomke more firmly in hand. He asked him to move his place of work from ETA in Grenchen to the head office in Biel. Thomke was given an office opposite Hayek's. Until then Thomke had striven to protect his finished watches domain as well as possible from outside. Yet Thomke's drive for independence had long been a thorn in Hayek's side. But Thomke proved very difficult to subdue. His teachers had attempted to do that earlier when they tried to turn him from a left-hander into a right-hander, without success. For Hayek, Thomke was also difficult to control because Thomke had a large information lead. Unlike Hayek, Thomke knew the watch business not only from reports and company figures but from the ground up. As a skilled watchmaker, he could look over his employees' shoulders at the workbench and show each of them how to do it right.

That was far from the only reason for the conflicts that developed between the two of them. Also in organisational matters, to which Thomke clearly accords more importance than Hayek, they were not in tune. For Hayek, the quality of the employees was the prime concern.

'When I go to a company with a bad organisation but talented people, I don't have to worry about its future. It is different when it's the other way round', Hayek used to say. The mistrust between Hayek and Thomke continued to grow. The disagreements had an increasingly negative impact on the mood of their closest colleagues. This led to the formation of followers who mistrusted each other or even fought in the company. It was the time of great intrigues. 'Everyone fought to belong to the inner circle of one of these two alpha-leaders, which naturally led to conflicts', tells a former long-serving member of the executive. The quarrel between the two strong men led increasingly to informal structures and so to new sources of friction. It was hardly possible to remain neutral without being worn down by both sides. Everyone was extremely careful what they said to whom. Anyone who belonged to the Thomke clan became suspicious to Hayek, and vice versa. The rumour mill kept turning. More and more often, Hayek would ask individual employees if Thomke had really said this or that. His suspicion was so extreme that he immediately reversed some of Thomke's decisions. One of the more extreme rumours that went around in the company at the time of the Iraq War was that Thomke had called Hayek a 'little Saddam Hussein'. Hayek soon got to hear about that, too.

The climate of uncertainty was sensed even by people who applied to work there. Anyone who went to be interviewed by Hayek, Thomke or even the Omega boss Fritz Ammann, gained the impression that each worked very differently from the other two, a former job applicant remembers. Tensions developed not only between Hayek and Thomke, but also between Thomke and his subordinate Ammann. When Thomke was occasionally bed-ridden with back pain at home in Grenchen, Ammann used his absence to strengthen his position in the company. He was seen going in and out of Hayek's office more and more often. The comeback was immediate: no sooner was Thomke back on his feet again than he publicly put his subordinate in his place. Ammann left the company shortly afterwards.

In 1990 Thomke received an honorary doctorate from ETH in Lausanne, six years before Hayek was accorded the same distinction by the University of Neuenburg. The news of the honour arrived at the traditional executive meeting at the Waldhaus Flims hotel in Bündner. When Thomke's colleagues heard this they immediately knew that the fuse was now finally lit. Hayek did not manage to conceal that this distinction granted to his colleague rankled deeply, for Hayek's cascade of honours only began a few years later. He only arrived at the last minute to the celebration at ETH in Lausanne. He limited his presence to the absolute minimum. He did not stay to take part in the banquet. What further deepened the quarrel between them was the fact that Hayek began increasingly often to take credit for other people's work in public and to present himself as 'Mister Swatch'. That offended Thomke and soon afterwards he began to say openly to his colleagues: 'I don't want to work with Hayek any more. I will resign.' When Hayek heard about his Director-General's imminent escape, a tug-of-war began between them about the terms of his departure.

The question now was whether it should be a resignation or a diplomatic separation. Hayek had absolutely nothing to gain from this departure creating huge turmoil. Nevertheless, certain rumours about Thomke's forthcoming retreat eventually leaked through to the press. When Hayek was asked by the *SonntagsZeitung* on 24 March 1991 whether it was true that Thomke was leaving, he answered categorically: 'That's not true. That's rubbish.' Thomke simply had rather a lot of work on his plate at the moment and was therefore being relieved. Some special assignments for the US market had been transferred to him. Also, he was going to devote himself to the Swatch-Car project.

The rift came more or less immediately afterwards. At the beginning of May 1991, SMH published a dry press release announcing that Thomke was leaving the group management on 1 June and his employment contract would be terminated. The board of directors had taken this decision unanimously. It was not very surprising that this decision turned out to be so conclusive. Hayek had always had the final say on the committee. Stephan Schmidheiny, the second most important member of the board of directors, did not much like Thomke anyway. Insiders say that the eastern Swiss investor had always considered Thomke rude and coarse. In fact, in disagreements Thomke goes more for the bludgeon than the rapier. He lacks the fine polish of the traditional business establishment. 'When Ernst Thomke first enters someone else's office, he does not open the door in the usual way but shoves it with his shoulder, almost with a swing of his body', remembers one of his former colleagues. Thomke is as gnarled as the huge iron statues made by the Bern artist Schang Hutter that stand in his garden in Grenchen, or the Bernhard Luginbühl statues at his holiday home in southern France.

It was a foregone conclusion that Thomke would come off worse in the quarrel with Hayek. In differences of opinion between owners and managers, the quarrel is usually resolved in favour of capital. 'There was not room for both of us and one or other had to go. I would have done exactly the same in Hayek's position', Thomke later realistically commented. But the sober impression that Thomke tried to give here did not characterise this separation. Instead, a further small-scale proxy war was subsequently kindled that looked to outsiders more like a painful farce. One year after the separation from Thomke, Hayek discovered a Swatch with a Rado dial in an auction catalogue. He suspected this was a prototype from the early days of Swatch, a unique piece that belonged to the company. The trail of this watch led to Thomke's daughter. It was nothing unusual for Thomke as the person in charge of the finished watches domain at the time to take an unsaleable test watch home from time to time. At the beginning he often tested these prototypes himself before passing them on to the laboratory for further testing. He later gave his daughter one of these test watches, which had no commercial value. The watch finally ended up with a gallery owner they knew in Zurich. He wanted to sell the watch at an auction and he had it included in the catalogue. Hayek discovered this and immediately brought a charge against person or persons unknown through his firm Rado. The sale of this Swatch at an auction finally led to a trial.

Today Hayek no longer likes to talk about Thomke, and Thomke is reluctant to talk about Hayek. Shortly after his departure, Thomke set up the so-called Spin-off Club. The loose-knit association still exists and today it has around three to four dozen members. At the beginning it consisted mainly of a few serious nostalgics who had left SMH with or after Thomke. Anyone who mentioned Hayek's name at an event or on an excursion had to put 50 francs into a kitty. Over time this gave rise to an impressive association fund that grew through an aggressive investment policy with the new economy bubble emerging on the stock exchange to around 250,000 francs. Since many of these internet companies crashed, there is not much of this left now. The only membership qualification for the association now is to have once worked with Thomke and to have left the Swatch Group payroll. The members meet around twice a year. The occasions range from eating asparagus or visiting the Liener museum in Appenzell to a cable-car ride on the Tschentenalp railway in Adelboden that was redeveloped by Thomke. The emotions have since abated. The individual member's relationship to Hayek no longer plays a part. Hardly anyone still disputes today his great service to the Swiss watch industry; deep down, probably not even Thomke.

7

The Great Man is Sufficient unto Himself – the Watch Magnate Reinforces his Dominance

A RIFT SOON DEVELOPED not only with Ernst Thomke but also with Stephan Schmidheiny, Hayek's partner in the pool agreement. The eastern Swiss industrialist turned away from his partner almost without any prior warning because he realised in the early 1990s that he could no longer play any constructive role at SMH. He left the investors' group and reduced his stake from 17 per cent to around 6 per cent in one year. Hayek was certainly no longer all that young when he took over the watch group and Schmidheiny had therefore repeatedly raised the question of succession arrangements in the board of directors. At the latest at retirement age, most entrepreneurs begin to look around for candidates to take over the operational management of their firms. However, Hayek kept postponing this step. Clearly, though, Schmidheiny was the only person to be concerned about this. The watch company was in such a good position that doubts were hardly ever expressed by the other shareholders.

The board of directors had always been a kind of 'rubber-stamping committee', says a former brand manager at the company. Matters of substance had rarely been discussed. As a brand manager, he was always called in at 11.30 a.m. to take part in the board meeting to report on his area of business. Soon afterwards they then proceeded to have lunch. Then the bank representatives were generally driven to the office by their chauffeurs. Not the multibillionaire Stephan Schmidheiny: he was the only one who almost always took the train. The long train journeys to his company Anova Holding in Hurden in the Schwyz canton seem to have given him ample opportunity to reflect on his commitment to SMH.

In fact, Hayek had to realise that Schmidheiny, who was known to be an active investor, would sooner or later draw his own conclusions.

At the end of 1993 he began to sell off part of his stake. 'Schmidheiny has left the pool agreement', a market trader shouted just before the holiday break at the Zurich stock exchange. Many investors, who did not know the full background to these security sales, must have gained the impression that the time had obviously come for investors to cash in. They followed him like sheep and sold their shares, too. In fact, Schmidheiny's capital investment had multiplied tenfold in around five years. Yet, as so often with rumours, the news of the eastern Swiss multibillionaire's exit was exaggerated. The pool agreement, consisting of around a dozen investors, still had four years left to run. However, a relaxation of the agreement enabled Schmidheiny to cede some of the votes to Hayek. Yet the investors did not really know what was going on, since the situation was hardly transparent to them. So the news of Schmidheiny's supposed exit caused a share price collapse in the SMH securities, and the stock market value quickly dropped by 2.5 billion francs. The market reaction to Schmidheiny's sale was a bitter disappointment not only to Hayek but also to many public shareholders. The small crash was even harder to understand when the company had achieved a fantastic profit margin. The fact that Schmidheiny at the time had contributed a substantial sum to this watch company had always been a strong seal of approval for the SMH security and a form of guarantee for investors. This benefit of this doubt was beginning to fade.

In time, Schmidheiny actually pulled out completely. He sold a portion of his registered shares not through the stock exchange but by exchanging them with Hayek for bearer shares. Since registered shares possess more voting power, Hayek could shore up his powerful position without having to pay a premium. Schmidheiny also contributed a stake at Martin Ebner's company Stillhalter Vision. At that time Hayek was still friendly with the financier, although not for much longer. The watch industrialist was less and less happy with Ebner's speculative deals.

On balance, the change in the shareholders had mainly a positive consequence for Hayek: now he was the biggest stakeholder. The share price collapse cannot have worried him too much as he considered his commitment as a long-term investment. Schmidheiny also left the board of directors. Hayek replaced him at the next general meeting with four new members – the Lindt & Sprüngli boss Ernst Tanner, the astronaut Claude Nicollier, the Davos Forum founder Klaus Schwab and his own daughter Nayla Hayek, who had previously mainly devoted herself to horse breeding. Observers agreed that Hayek was seeking to further strengthen his position on the board of directors with the choice of these people, for these were all people who would never be able to stand up to him.

In the case of Klaus Schwab, though, Hayek had been mistaken. The Geneva professor tried to play a very active role in the board of directors and kept putting forward new proposals. However, these were not well received by Hayek. Very soon the two of them fell out, and Schwab resigned as Vice-President. Hayek would not be told anything by anyone on the board of directors, according to the founder of the World Economic Forum when he later explained his departure. Hayek argued back and accused Schwab of a lack of industrial flair. The watch magnate built up his dominant position over the next few years. He gradually increased his financial stake by seizing every favourable opportunity to buy shares.

Hayek had clearly backed the right horse. The watch company that was now renamed the Swatch Group recorded profits growth that constantly moved in the double-digit region. Business was running very smoothly, though, in the rest of the Swiss watch industry. The Japanese companies Citizen and Seiko had finally lost their dominance on the global markets. The rise in the value of the yen was giving the Japanese problems and in the Land of the Rising Sun the mood of crisis was deepening. In terms of units sold, Japan certainly still held first place in the mid-1990s, but in value terms the Swiss manufacturers accounted for over half of the global sales.

With the final breakthrough of Swatch on all the major markets and the reorganisation of Omega, Hayek had moved one further critical step closer to his strategic goal. Swatch was at the peak of its success in the mid-1990s with an annual production of well over 20 million units, and it contributed around one billion francs to the turnover. The watch group was strong at both the top and the base of the price pyramid, which had been achieved by revolutionising the sales strategy. Hayek appealed to the consumer in a completely new way. Instead of praising his products with the traditional, factual sales arguments, he put everything in emotional terms. Hayek used to say that he was not selling a consumer item but communicating a message to the buyer.

Today chronometers are no longer sold, as in the postwar years, with ordinary statements such as 'The X watch is the most precise and accurate in the world'. Since the introduction of electronics, individual watches have been almost indistinguishable in their utility value. The regularity of the quartz oscillations in the movement has made all electronic watches, whether they are made in Hong Kong or Switzerland, more or less accurate. Of course, there are striking differences in design, price and functions. Yet the new nature of this consumer product led Hayek to seek for the Swatch something that took place outside it: an attractive message. The sales slogan ever since has emphasised the highest quality at the lowest price and challenges and fun in life. The Swatch is not a successor product of the earlier Roskopf concept and not just a 'poor people's watch'. To convey its quality as a lifestyle product, over many years the Swatch team tried to fill the message with all kinds of fun activities, with sports and dance events and other topics.

At Omega, Hayek had to adopt a very different approach. The former all-purpose appearance with the correspondingly traditional face from the old SSIH days was removed, and it was radically transformed into a prestige brand. Omega stands for 'beauty and elegance', which has been the slogan since then. In 1995, Hayek hired Cindy Crawford to give the message credibility and to promote it internationally, which established the ambassador concept. James Bond also wore an Omega, a Seamaster. And even in the latest Bond film, the leading actor Daniel Craig is displaying an Omega on his wrist again. The list of stars who have since plugged Omega has reached an impressive length.

Once the highest and the lowest price segments were well secured, now the middle section was due for a reorganisation. Hayek aimed to become strong in every layer of the 'wedding cake', as the watch price-pyramid is called in the internal company jargon. In the middle price segment too, consumers were targeted at the emotional level. Here, though, the restructurings did not have such great repercussions. Hayek never paid the same attention to brands like Mido, Certina or Tissot as he did to Omega, Breguet or Swatch. Although he constantly says that all the brands are important to him, this price segment is still not as strategically important to him; after all, it also contributes much less to the added value.

To realise fully his concept of emotionalising in sales, Hayek had to gain a stronger influence on the distribution. He therefore began to concentrate on building up his own network of shops. Hayek tried to bring the advertising under his control and to increase its effectiveness.

This strategy was most consistently implemented in the USA. There the Swatch was soon sold exclusively in its own stores. The New York subsidiary then managed to achieve phenomenal records with occasionally almost 85,000 watches sold in a year. In the luxury brands sector, Hayek began to build up his own distribution network with the so-called Tourbillon shops. From 2000, one new Omega flagship store opened almost every few months, for instance in Moscow, Shanghai and Geneva. The specialist trade was not at all happy about this new competition. On the Zurich Bahnhofstraße especially, this course of action caused a stir. On the most expensive shopping street in Switzerland, fierce complaints were made against the watch magnate behind closed doors. A few worried specialist dealers painted the ghost of the shop dying on the wall. Hayek tried to reassure his buyers that the new concept was taking nothing away from anyone, but instead reviving the market. He argued that the innovation would lead to additional sales with them. To demonstrate that he did not want to embark on any kind of collision course with the specialist dealers, Hayek founded a joint Omega store with the firm Gübelin AG on the Zurich Bahnhofstraße. Meanwhile, the Swatch Group had started to run similar joint ventures with other dealers as well. Hayek was to be proved right. Unlike the retail trade, in watch sales there is no question of shops closing down. In the luxury sector, the lion's share of the revenue is still handled today by the independent specialist trade; only around one tenth of the sales are made through the Omega flagship stores. For Hayek, they are primarily a marketing tool.

Every new store opening is therefore turned into an event with public appeal. So the inauguration of the Omega shop in Geneva was attended by the Oscar-winning actress Nicole Kidman. With so much publicity, Hayek's role as a top seller in the Swiss watch industry had to draw increasing attention not only in Europe but also in the USA. There, too, the unmistakable ticking of Swiss watches was heard again. The malicious articles about the crisis-stricken Swiss watch industry were long gone and it was once again being considered as an exemplary model. In an interview with the *Harvard Business Review*, Hayek was asked what conclusions he drew from the successful recovery of the Swiss watch industry. As probably the best-known Swiss business leader abroad, he said what he was constantly to say in the following years: the success of the Swatch shows that even in high-wage countries such as Switzerland it is possible to manufacture high-quality goods at low cost for mass consumption. If this mass production is abandoned and relocated to low-wage countries, the USA and Europe inevitably risked losing their skills. Losing control over strategically important components would simultaneously jeopardise the production of high-quality goods. This way the industrial countries would gamble with not only their prosperity but in the end also their supremacy.

Hayek draws parallels between the earlier crisis in the Swiss watch industry and the bleak situation of the European and American car industry. Like the watch industry then, car manufacturers neglected the lower market segment. The sales crisis that hit the American car industry especially hard in the second half of 2008 proves Hayek right. Detroit fled with heavy gas-guzzlers into ever-higher price segments, where the air gets ever thinner, which is not only because of protective environmental measures. Hayek says that the manufacture of premium-quality cars can only be secured in the long term if it manages to strengthen its competitiveness in the cheaper vehicles sector. Otherwise the manufacturers in the industrialising countries will be able to exploit this weakness in future.

Jobs in the industrial countries can only be preserved in the long run by reducing the proportion of labour costs to total costs. Hayek has shown, with the example of his watch company, that this is possible. At the beginning, labour costs at SMH still constituted 30 per cent of the total cost of the watch production. Certainly, the wage bill has since risen considerably in absolute terms. Nevertheless, it was possible to reduce the proportion of the wages in the Swatch Group to less than 10 per cent. Today the capital costs – the total expenditure on machines, robotics and technology – are carrying much more weight. Hayek has proved that a restructuring of the production apparatus in the direction of increasing added value is also possible without cutting wages. Salaries in his factories are in the good industrial average. Hayek achieved his savings primarily by optimising and automating the production process to increase productivity. He could thus largely compensate for the cost disadvantage in comparison with the low-wage countries.

Hayek has an excellent head for figures. It is one of his strengths to draw the right conclusions at lightning speed from a large, confusing jumble of numbers. Before he handed over operational responsibility to his son Nick, the sales figures for all the brands from the previous month always had to be on his desk on the sixth day of the month, with the profit and loss account two weeks later. When the finance people and the brand managers had to trot up to the senior man for the budget meeting, they always entered this appointment in the diary in red. That was a day like no other. As they walked into Seevorstadt, the executives' blood pressure would rise noticeably. The Chief Executive today still always has a bulky, hand-sized pocket calculator in front of him, with which he examines the figures put in front of him in the smallest detail. In an A4-size large leather folder he has all the important key figures to hand. He does not need a computer – he can tell even without one where there are still hidden possibilities for savings. With this consistent cost management, Hayek managed to prevail over the cheaper competition from the Far East.

Some business leaders long believed that Switzerland as an industrial location only still had a chance against the competition from the industrialising countries in the highest price segment. There was a widespread view that the country was predestined to develop into a service society, and there was an extremely pessimistic assessment of the prospects for the industrial base. Hayek fiercely objected: banks and insurance companies only had a long-term future if the manufacturing sector were maintained and further developed. A slow death for Switzerland as an industrial zone along the lines of the dwindling traditional firms Rieter, Sulzer or Georg Fischer would also ultimately endanger jobs in the service companies. He is convinced that banks and insurance companies could not survive without a manufacturing industry.

However, Hayek does not so resolutely champion Switzerland as a manufacturing base out of pure patriotism. As a watch industrialist he has no choice but to rely on the homeland base. He can only produce goods in Switzerland – there is no question of relocating production in grand style for the watch industry. The credibility of the 'Swiss-made' origin designation is not just a trump card for this industry but rather a question of survival. The label is still one of the most important sales arguments.

The 'Swiss-made' label cannot be had for free, though. The automation and robotisation of Swiss factories, especially to the extent that they have been taken for the Swatch, is a costly matter. If the expensive high-tech machines used now worked for no more than eight hours a day, the sums would not work out. The industrial robots in the Swatch production incur capital costs for the company even when they are not in operation. To have these machines running round the clock requires supervisory staff. At first, though, night working in the industry was very limited. The Federal Council had declined a corresponding request by ETA for night work in 1984 because it would have contravened one of the agreements signed by Switzerland at the International Labour Organisation (ILO). The more Hayek invested in the machinery for parts production, the more urgent it became for him to solve this problem. Hayek had meanwhile invested around 100 million francs in chips manufacturing in Marin in Neuenburg. One single workstation there costs several hundred thousand francs. When the Federal Council cancelled the ILO agreement concerned at the beginning of the 1990s, Hayek went straight to the employee organisations. He managed to persuade the trade unions to adopt a compromise solution with which both the staff and EM Marin, as a manufacturer of specific integrated circuits, could live. The watch magnate from then on had a free hand not only at the top on the board of directors. At the grass roots too, hardly any more obstacles were put in his way by the trade unions.

8

Enough is Never Enough – Hayek's Luxury Problem and his Move into the Top League

HAYEK COULD, IN FACT, now have retired gently. His watch group was on top form. He had achieved almost everything there was to achieve – prosperity, prestige and personal fulfilment. Yet it was not in Hayek's nature to stop there. With Omega he did not, in fact, yet belong to the exclusive club of the top range, the group of ultra-expensive luxury watches. Omega is certainly one of the high-end brands, but it is not a top-league player like Patek Philippe or Audemars Piguet. These Geneva brands manufacture watches that cost a fortune. For the Patek Philippe 5207P model, for example, one of this firm's most complicated watches, you have to shell out 700,000 francs. It is a watch with all the refinements. The platinum case contains a highly complicated tourbillon to increase its accuracy, a perpetual calendar that includes leap years and a minute repeater. Today even an Omega Hour Vision in white gold from the De Ville model range can easily cost 30,000 francs, but despite this very high price for ordinary mortals Omega is not one of the top brands. The launch of even more expensive models was not an option, though, for Hayek. If he had tried to reach the top with the company flagship, he would have diversified too far. The price spectrum between the individual models would have stretched too wide. Such a strategy would have swallowed up an enormous advertising budget.

Yet it was still Hayek's ambition to belong to the exclusive club as well. It did not escape his notice that the complicated mechanical watches from Geneva had been in especially strong demand since the end of the 1980s. In the luxury watches segment, a real gold-digging mood was arising. It turned out that sales of extremely expensive watches suffer much less than the middle and lower price range in recessionary times. Also, the margins are much higher.

Hayek tried to launch his own luxury brand under the name Louis Brand. This was the name of the man who had founded Omega in 1848. It was also steeped in history because that was the year in which the Swiss Federal State was established. Yet the launch of this new watch was a flop. Who but a historically knowledgeable watch freak has heard of Louis Brand? Creating an entirely new brand from scratch is difficult and costly. For Hayek, the only alternative now was to buy a well-known prestige brand and so connect with a tradition. But he had no illusions about this because the possibilities were very limited. When asked which luxury brand he was most interested in, he always immediately put off the question: 'Either these high-end brands that are a possibility are not for sale or they are much too expensive.' Hayek did not want to get carried away in an adventure with incalculable risks. He was patient.

When he was given an opportunity to buy the firm Ebel in La Chaux-de-Fonds, which had gone into a tailspin, Hayek politely declined. He considered the price being asked totally extortionate. The brand was eventually bought by LMVH Moët Hennessy–Louis Vuitton. At the Paris luxury goods company, money had long since ceased to be a major factor in acquisitions. Hayek also had the possibility of buying Chaumet, which was also swallowed up by LVMH, but he felt that this brand did not fit with SMH.

Hayek was looking for something truly special with which he could sensibly extend his wide brands portfolio. When the Mannesmann brands IWC, Jaeger LeCoultre and Lange & Söhne came up for sale, Hayek expressed an interest – these firms could have been easily integrated into his strategy. Yet the Mannesmann parent company, the British firm Vodafone, gave Hayek the cold shoulder. The Swiss–South African company Richemont surpassed the Swatch Group with a fundamentally more attractive offer. The sum paid by Richemont is said to have been more than ten times the annual turnover of these three firms. Such a high sale price was highly unusual in the industry; generally in acquisitions, double the turnover amount was paid. As a cost-conscious entrepreneur, Hayek did not want to join this race, in which each tried to outbid the other with an even more lucrative offer. He would also have dearly liked to take on Patek Philippe or Rolex. However, he was always aware that these pearls would hardly ever be up for sale. Also, such a financial feat would have been beyond his possibilities. Hayek would have been forced to go against his principles: he would have had to call on the banks for help. That was something he was determined to avoid.

Yet in 1992 the moment arrived: Hayek bought the Blancpain brand. Finally he could set a gold crown on his SMH group. Blancpain is the oldest watch brand in Switzerland; the company was founded in 1735. Strictly speaking, Blancpain had already belonged to Hayek's company before, but at that time it was merely a discontinued brand that had ceased production. During the watch crisis Blancpain had almost been put on ice. The finished watch company SSIH had taken over the brand, without ever daring to try to revive it, until finally Jean-Claude Biver came along and gave the princess the kiss of life. Biver was then head of marketing at Omega. He had long planned to go independent. When, in 1982, he stumbled on this deeply traditional name in the drawers of the SSIH head office in Biel, he snatched the opportunity. He bought the brand rights from his employer at the knockdown price of 18,000 francs. With his friend Frédéric Piguet, owner of the Piguet manufacturing site for mechanical movements, he built a new watch factory in the Waadtland Jura. For this they recruited a few older watchmakers who still mastered the craft in the sector of high-quality mechanical chronometers. Since the introduction of electronics, there had been a lack of qualified younger workers in this occupation. Biver and Piguet soon achieved great success. After ten years – having bought out his partner who had left – and with around 130 employees, Biver was generating a turnover of around 50 million francs. His illustrious customers included the Sultan of Brunei, one of the richest men in the world. But many Middle Eastern oil sheiks also spent their petro-dollars on the expensive Blancpain watches.

In time Biver realised that his medium-sized company had limited development potential and he would have much better prospects under the auspices of a financially strong company. He therefore approached Hayek with an offer. Hayek did not hesitate for long and he bought Blancpain from the young entrepreneur for an estimated 30 million francs. Hayek had another thought at the back of his mind there. He was almost as interested in the firm Piguet that belonged to it. For the movements production of the luxury range with its valuable associated skills, Hayek may have forked out an equally large sum. Today Piguet produces movements not only for Hayek's luxury brands but also for third parties such as Vacheron Constantin. At last SMH was established at the pinnacle of the watches segment. From Blancpain to Swatch, Hayek covered the whole product spectrum and all the price ranges. Along with ETA, which makes the electronic mass-produced watch movements, he now also had a manufacturing site for highly complicated mechanical movements.

Not only Hayek's SMH but the whole watch industry was in flux in the 1990s. The crisis was overcome. One company after another changed ownership. The sports watch manufacturer TAG Heuer was also bought up by the French luxury goods group LVMH. It was only a matter of time before Hayek would grasp another favourable opportunity. 'We always have money available for acquisitions. When I want to seize a good opportunity, I don't rely on the banks', he told me at the time in an interview. Actually the watch magnate had around one billion francs in his war chest. In 1986, he acquired the Paris brand Léon Hatot. The brand is known for jewellery and jewellery watches in the art deco style.

Hayek landed the really big coup one year later, when he took over the firm Montres Breguet from the investment company Investcorp. Industry insiders talked at the time of a sale price of 300 million francs. But Breguet was certainly worth that. Today it is the pearl among the Swiss luxury brands. Strictly speaking, the brand has a French rather than a Swiss origin. The company was founded in Paris by Abraham-Louis Breguet, from Neuenburg, in 1775. The group today owns the production company Nouvelle Lemania in L'Orient, which manufactures watches for the Breguet brand and mechanical movements for third-party clients, as well as Valdar SA, which specialises in micro-mechanical components. It was only in 1976 that the company moved from Paris to the Vallée de Joux, which is also home to Hayek's luxury brand Blancpain. The area around the Lac de Joux is a real watch mecca. ETA, the electronic watch movements manufacturer, also runs a factory there. The valley is occasionally called 'Hayek valley' by local residents.

When Hayek took over Breguet, the company was heavily in debt. Many industry experts strongly advised him against the purchase, but Hayek would not be scared off. He was firmly convinced that this brand contained even greater potential than Blancpain. He took over the operational management personally in order to lick the company into shape as fast as possible. Hayek made himself President of the board of directors, CEO, head of marketing, and head of production and development in the personal union, and in a few years he led the company to flourish again. Today, Breguet is still Hayek's favourite child among the group's 19 brands. When he took over the factory, the company had orders for just 4,000 watches; 18 months later, there were already 12,000. Today in L'Orient over 30,000 high-quality watches are produced a year. The sales have been showing double-digit growth rates for some years. The watches produced include a few especially exclusive individual pieces, models that are manufactured using the same method as the firm's founder Breguet himself.

A few years ago Hayek had the opportunity to acquire one of these Breguet watches made 200 years ago for about one million euros. When the Sultan of Oman noticed the valuable piece Hayek drew out of his pocket while they were sharing a meal, he was so taken with it that he wanted to buy it from him immediately. Hayek did not want to part with his newly acquired piece of jewellery at any price, not even to the Arab ruler who was one of his best customers. Yet Hayek promised the Sultan that he would have the watch recreated for him. Qabus bin Said was extremely pleased and immediately ordered five. Whether the Sultan has actually worn all these five watches is only known if at all to the attendants who can observe him very closely in his five palatial homes. But that was probably hardly his intention when he bought them. For a Breguet watch today is not merely an article of daily use but also a valuable capital investment. Someone who acquires one of these fine chronometers for 300,000 francs has a good chance of being able to resell it a few years later at Sotheby's auction house for twice that amount.

It is questionable whether this deal with the Sultan would have happened if Breguet had still belonged to Investcorp. It seems highly improbable. First, the managers then working for the short-termist financier would probably never have had the idea of recreating this historic watch. Second, as certainly highly paid but relatively anonymous employees, they would hardly have been on such good terms with the Sultan as Hayek. The investment company had in any case failed to exploit the potential that lay in this traditional brand. In accordance with its objective as a financial company, Investcorp was only seeking the highest possible capital returns. Unlike Hayek, it had no emotional connection with the product and none of its backing investors was a specialist in this industry. So the time fairly soon came when the financial company wanted to get rid of its investment again to cash in. Investcorp had bought Breguet from the jewellery firm Chaumet in 1987, without knowing where the journey would lead. The investment company had no connection with the illustrious past of this brand name.

However, Hayek put his heart and soul into doing everything he could to revive the old days. The Breguet clientele over the last 200 years had in fact included not only rich ordinary mortals but also kings, emperors and popes. The list of Breguet patrons includes Marie Antoinette, Louis XVI, Napoleon Bonaparte, Tsar Alexander I, George III of England, Queen Victoria, Pope Pius VII, Arthur Rubinstein, Winston Churchill and King Faruk of Egypt, to name just a few of the most famous historical figures. Publicity for Breguet can even be found in world literature. The watch brand was mentioned by Honoré de Balzac in his *Comédie Humaine*, Alexandre Dumas in *The Count of Monte Cristo*, and also named by Pushkin and Stendhal in their works. The poem in which Pushkin praises Breguet watches is still studied by pupils in Russian schools today.

Hayek skilfully deploys this history for publicity purposes. So he established a watch museum especially for Breguet at the Place Vendôme in Paris. Almost all the luxury watch brands are represented in the exclusive specialist shops on this square around the five-star Ritz hotel. The collection is managed by Emmanuel Breguet, the youngest direct descendant of the firm's founder. On the other hand, the masterpiece, number 160, the 'Marie Antoinette', is on display in the museum of Islamic art in Tel Aviv. In the Breguet museum there is only a reproduction of this watch on display. It is a pocket watch with all the trimmings – a leap-year indicator, a moon-phase indicator and further refinements – which Breguet manufactured for Queen Marie Antoinette. But money is not everything in life. The French queen never actually got to see the piece of jewellery – she was executed before the watch was completed. Hayek has had the pocket watch reconstructed down to the smallest detail from old drawings. The watch, now christened 'Marie Antoinette', is therefore not a copy in any sense, as he emphasised in 2008 at its presentation to the Basel international watch trade fair.

Hayek understands brilliantly how to keep reviving the aura surrounding the brand with anecdotes and legends. For the 200th anniversary of the day on which Abraham-Louis Breguet received his order in person from the French Interior Minister for his tourbillon regulator watch, he organised a grand celebration. This was not held in any old luxury hotel – no, the watch magnate had his eye on the courtyard of the Château Versailles. Around 600 carefully selected VIPs were invited, including the German Interior Minister Otto Schily and the Greek singer Nana Mouskouri. Hayek laid on a midnight dinner with foie gras, Bresse chicken and verbena sorbet in the largest room in the Château. The crowning glory was a large fireworks display.

With nostalgia alone, though, no deals can be made. Hayek therefore seeks to forge a connection not only with tradition but also with Abraham-Louis Breguet's pioneering spirit. 'Breguet revolutionised the art of watchmaking', was how he praised the Swiss inventor who moved to France at Versailles. It was Hayek's goal from the outset to make Breguet the most innovative luxury brand. In this he has since undoubtedly succeeded. For this, however, he had to move away from the 'small is beautiful' philosophy that dominates in the luxury segment. The idea that a luxury brand has to be managed like a craftsman's workshop and may not seek to generate high revenues is, in his view, outmoded. Hayek wanted to make clear that a luxury brand, too, must move with the times and be innovative if it is to continue developing. Breguet therefore now generates a revenue of over half a billion francs. Nevertheless, these watches are of course not ordinary industrially produced products. Almost everything today in a gold or platinum Breguet watch is still hand-made. Even the few machine-made parts are still refined and decorated by hand at the end.

In fact, Abraham-Louis Breguet himself was far ahead of his time. He had also steered his company on a path of expansion. He did not limit himself to the French market, but very soon opened a branch in St Petersburg. The brand has always had a very close connection with Russia. Once when the Russian Tsar came to Paris, Breguet is said to have invited him to dinner with a group of officers. That is another story that Hayek likes to tell in company. One of the Russian officers who accompanied the Tsar put his Breguet watch on the table during the meal. Suddenly the valuable piece disappeared. To identify the thief, they closed all the doors at the Tsar's behest. Then one by one each officer had to empty his trouser pockets and lay the contents on the table. One of them, just as his turn came, suddenly drew his pistol and shot himself. A message was found on a piece of paper that he left behind. Here the officer explained the reason for his suicide: he actually had a Breguet watch in his pocket. This belonged to him, though. However, he could not have borne any suspicion falling on him and possibly being accused of stealing it. Therefore he had taken his own life. Later the missing watch was found in the gap between the back and the seat of the chair of the person supposed to have been robbed. A fine story – even if it is not true, it is at least beautifully told. It is almost made for creating legends around the luxury piece in the way Hayek loves. Even today the brand is still one of the most sought-after luxury watches among the new rich upper class in Russia. One of around a dozen Breguet shops worldwide is in Moscow.

Just one year after the Breguet takeover, Hayek resumed his shopping spree. Next he acquired the high-end Saxon brand Glashütte Original. This watch manufacturer founded in 1845 also has a turbulent history. After initially producing mainly wristwatches and pocket watches, the firm specialised in watches designed for the Navy and the Air Force before the Second World War. In the communist-ruled GDR days, the state tried to rebuild the company on the wreckage of the war. Yet the watches were only sold in the Warsaw Pact countries. Most of the buyers came from the ranks of East German party officials. The brand only experienced an upsurge after the fall of the Berlin Wall and the privatisation of the economy. Since then, high-quality watches with a tourbillon and perpetual calendar in the 4,000–200,000 francs price bracket have been manufactured again. Hayek invested a great deal of money in the business and achieved double-digit sales growth by substantially increasing the export share. The purchase of the Waadtland luxury brand Jacquet Droz in the same year was then far less important. The turnover of this brand was in the single-millions region. Under Hayek's direction, the company is also developing very well.

As we know, the appetite increases with eating. The success soon gave Hayek the idea of expanding into the jewellery area. Watches and jewellery have many points in common. Expensive watches are partly acquired as items of jewellery. A luxury watch is essentially a piece of jewellery. The jewellery market is especially attractive because its global volume is four times greater than the watch industry and it clearly also achieves higher growth rates and higher margins.

This was new territory for Hayek. Jewellery had till then been bought by consumers more for its design than the brand. The situation has since changed. Since Hayek turned it into a branding business at the beginning of the new century with his company 'Dress your body', the brand share in jewellery has doubled. The jewellery collections designed and made in-house at Swatch, Breguet, Omega, Léon Hatot and the licensed brand cK Calvin Klein are highly successful. The Omega and Swatch stores are proving to be excellent platforms for presenting jewellery along with watches, and jewellery in these shops now constitutes up to one fifth of the total turnover. Hayek wants to increase the share gradually to one tenth of the company turnover.

With cK, a brand under which almost everything is sold today from watches to boxer shorts, Hayek is moving further into the territory of luxury goods companies such as Louis Vuitton or Gucci. Their product range is very wide and extends from watches to handbags. But Hayek does not want to be lumped in with these names. '*Il y a des horlogers qui pètent au-dessus de leur cul*', was how he once mocked these competitors, without naming any names. Translated decently, this vulgar expression means that there are watch brands that claim to be something more than they truly are. In his view, consumers today distinguish too little between the brands that manufacture their own watches and companies that sell perfumes, handbags and a dozen other things besides and then also bring watches alongside them into the product range. Actually, brands such as Gucci would not be able to manufacture complete watches themselves without the Swatch Group. The components used by these brands almost all come from Hayek's company.

A few years ago Hayek caused these fashion brands some serious embarrassment. Just before Christmas 2007, his son Nick made a particularly clever move to reinforce the bridge that had been built into the jewellery market. Hayek junior got the leading American jewellery brand Tiffany on board as a strategic partner. The Swatch Group acquired the right to produce luxury watches under this brand from that point on.

9
Who Dares Wins – the Setbacks in Hayek's Career

E VEN SUCCESSFUL ENTREPRENEURS such as Hayek must bear in mind that they will occasionally make the wrong decision and fall flat on their faces. When the production facility for the Smart Car in Hambach opened in 1997, Hayek even asked the German Chancellor Helmut Kohl and the French President Jacques Chirac if they would write a 'right to fail' for entrepreneurs into the European constitution. Of course, it was not an entirely serious suggestion. All Hayek meant was that a new risk-taking culture was needed in Europe. His credo is that 'Only someone who takes a risk on something with a new idea can succeed.' Hayek has always remained true to this established principle of successful entrepreneurship – who dares wins.

After a few years, the watch company was already so profitable that Hayek could easily afford to take certain calculated risks. He initially believed that the time would come when the potential of the watch business would be largely exhausted. He therefore sought some new development opportunities in other consumer goods sectors. Today, Hayek takes a much more positive view of the long-term prospects of the watch business: until everyone in China and India has a watch on their wrist, the Swatch Group has further good development possibilities in its core business.

Hayek saw new opportunities arising mainly in telecommunications and car manufacturing. Hayek had already gained some experience of the car industry in previous years as a consultant and he still maintained good relations with the industry. However, it was specifically with his car project that he was to experience one of his greatest disappointments as an entrepreneur. Hayek never tried to gloss over this failure. 'My hybrid car was a flop. I chose the wrong firm for it', he once candidly admitted to the financial magazine *Bilanz*. He is convinced that the decision to work with Mercedes was taken too hastily at the time – he should have mustered more patience to find the right partner.

The less than innovative German car industry was not actually the right partner for what was then a revolutionary plan to develop an eco-friendly small car. Later the Japanese approached the European and American car industry and carried out Hayek's idea of the combined electric and petrol engine. Toyota was the first car manufacturer to achieve the breakthrough with the Prius. The hybrid model established in the upper mid-range became a great success.

Yet at the time Hayek's vision was much more ambitious. Originally his Swatch-Mobil equipped with an eco-friendly hybrid propulsion incorporated a completely new mobility concept. Public and private transport should be dovetailed together. At only 3 litres per 100 kilometres, Hayek's small city car would also have consumed one third less petrol than the Toyota Prius. Hayek explained his idea as follows: 'Instead of the current oversized car with four or five seats, all that is necessary is a car with room for two passengers and a crate of beer.' Existing vehicles are much bigger than is required to meet our mobility needs. On average, one car is occupied by only 1.2 people. Transporting one or two people does not require a ton-heavy metal crate that is ten times the bodyweight of the passengers, consumes disproportionate amounts of fuel and emits an enormous volume of noxious substances. Petrol consumption depends not only on the type of engine but also on the weight of the vehicle. It is also easier to find a parking space with a small car of this kind.

Thus Hayek wanted to produce the lightest possible vehicle with an optimal energy footprint. There was no question of a purely electric car. There were already enough models of these. Because of their dependence on electrical sockets and their short range, these electric cars proved to have little market appeal. Hayek decided on the hybrid solution – a car with an engine that runs on both electricity and petrol. He had the electric motor and battery developed by his newly established SMH Automobile SA in collaboration with the engineering school in Biel.

In this car the petrol engine initially powered a generator. This provided an 80 kilogramme battery with electricity. From the battery, each of the four wheels was propelled by a 10 kilowatt electric motor. This car would have been around 200 kilogrammes heavier than the conventional Smart Car that is on the market today, but it would have consumed around 2 litres less petrol.

The objectives that Hayek had set himself with this project as a pioneer who was new to the industry were very ambitious. Like the Swatch, the new car was to embody the highest quality, the lowest price, and challenges and fun in life. Therefore he initially called it the Swatch-Mobil. The business plan anticipated car sales of 200,000 for the first year, to reach break-even point in the third. Hayek considered this project as much more than a pilot scheme; in his view the car division should in fact have contributed around 5 billion francs to the SMH Group turnover after 10–15 years. Hayek wanted to become as strong in the car industry as in the watch business within this timespan.

Hayek had realised, however, that he could not achieve this breakthrough solely by his own efforts. To construct a factory, an international distribution and a repair system, he needed help from the car industry. So in 1990 he went in search of a partner, taking one of several prototypes that he had had built at various secret locations. Hayek met with strong interest from the VW chairman Daniel Goeudevert. Goeudevert was even more impressed by this idea when the watch entrepreneur had taken over the project management personally and put his entire reputation on the line. Yet the partnership with Volkswagen Wolfsburg broke down after just one year, which was due to a change of management that also brought a change in the company philosophy. Goeudevert, who was open to environmental projects, was driven out of the company by 'gas-foot' Ferdinand Piëch. Having newly gained power, the Porsche grandson had no time for this Swiss watch entrepreneur's new, unsporty little car, and he treated Hayek with contempt: 'I could only tell him that I don't want to build a watch and I don't need any car from him … to me it was a elephant's roller-skate', Piëch wrote in his autobiography. He was convinced that market needs could be much better met by fast and stylish models. The fact that what he saw as a crazy idea also came from an outsider to the industry made it implausible for him anyway. For Piëch, only car engineers were capable of building a roadworthy vehicle.

So Hayek had to look for a new partner. He soon found one in Mercedes-Benz. The two companies jointly launched the Micro Compact Car AG (MCC). Actually, Hayek would have liked to control the majority of the share capital but, as the car manufacturer, Mercedes had the upper hand and wanted 51 per cent. The watch boss had to be content with the rest. He put his Swatch manager Hans-Jürg

Schär on the three-strong management board. The former central bank boss, Fritz Leutwiler, also sat on the MCC board of directors. Yet as a counterweight to the major partner, Leutwiler, contrary to Hayek's expectations, was no help to him as he died shortly after his selection. So for once the watch magnate had to make do with the passenger seat in the journey with Mercedes. He did not at all like this rather unaccustomed role because he had increasing difficulty bringing his ideas into the project.

Hayek certainly knew who he was up against. He knew the corporate culture of the car industry very well from his previous consultancy contracts. He realised that a conservative spirit prevails in this industry, and yet he had not reckoned with the collaboration becoming so laborious. Hayek had imagined a production on a similar module system to the Swatch. Hayek saw strong similarities and many parallels between cars and watches. Both were consumer goods with emotional associations for the buyer, he tried to explain to his partners. Yet that was a completely new perspective for the car manufacturer. The Swiss had a tough time making their arguments, especially as they were not car manufacturing experts. They were also totally unfamiliar with the large sums of money with which this industry operated. There they calculated in billions, rather than millions as in the watch industry. Many of Hayek's suggestions fell on deaf ears. The frictions began even with finding it a name. The name Swatch-Car that was planned in the joint venture contract was very quickly dropped. Mercedes insisted on the name Smart. It was soon forgotten that it was to have been called the Swatch-Car.

Nevertheless, the MCC car project was taken forward, though on a different level from that originally planned. Mercedes established that the MCC initially began with the production of a conventional 55 hp Smart with a 0.6 litre three-cylinder petrol engine, and Hayek's eco-model was only to roll off the production line two years later. The production company was opened in Hambach in France, rather than Switzerland as Hayek had hoped. An illustrious band of guests travelled to the opening ceremony, including Helmut Kohl, Jacques Chirac and Cindy Crawford. Yet the television crews were less interested in the high-ranking politicians and models than the cigar-puffing Nicolas Hayek, although the production of his hybrid had been put on the back-burner and Hayek was actually no longer setting the pace. The watch magnate was simply the more attractive interviewee: unlike the politicians and the Mercedes managers, the talented communicator dished out his usual snappy statements to the media.

Hayek in front of a Smart car.

The media attention was some small comfort for Hayek. The car whose production launch was being celebrated here had little in common with his eco-car. Even the price was far above the original 10,000-franc guideline. There was not very much new about the small car apart from its compact construction and new-style design, and it also experienced a mass of teething problems. The Smart failed the moose test; it tipped into the curve in evasion manoeuvres, and the driving stability was completely inadequate. After these problems were overcome, the first Smart with a traditional petrol engine finally left the factory in 1998.

Another bitter disappointment for Hayek was the bold expansion strategy adopted by the car manufacturer. Mercedes steered through an expansion of not only the model range but also the overseas route. Both required additional investments and the car manufacturer massively increased its contribution of share capital. This reduced Hayek's stake to 19 per cent, and he was now even more clearly in a minority position. Hayek's interest slowly dwindled as nothing corresponded to his original idea any more. For SMH, as a small company in relation to Mercedes, the risk anyway slowly became too high. Hayek feared that the car project might have a negative impact on the profit situation at SMH. So he put on the brakes and sold his shares to Mercedes. Investors made the same judgement of the situation as Hayek. They took a positive view of his step and the price of the SMH title rose sharply. The watch group had by then already invested around 300 million francs in its involvement in this other industry. By selling his stake, Hayek released another 150 million francs. In retrospect, it turned out that he had done the right thing by getting out. The Smart was anything but a successful product for a long time. Only ten years later, when the millionth vehicle rolled off the production line in Hambach in France, did the car yield a profit.

Although Hayek's car was never built, the watch group benefited hugely from the publicity generated by this tiny car. Whenever people talked about the Swatch-Mobil, the Swatch-Car and afterwards the Smart, this inspired an association with Hayek's Swatch Group in consumers. Another ten years later, on the anniversary of Smart production, the German press was celebrating the watch magnate as the instigator of this vehicle. His former partners dutifully thanked him: 'Without Hayek, the Smart project would never have happened', said Jürgen Hubbert, the long-standing Mercedes boss. Actually, the car company now has a cult car in its model range similar to the early Mini from the Swinging Sixties, not least thanks to Hayek.

Even when he left MCC, it was clear that Hayek's car dream was still alive. The watch boss later went to see the Mercedes managers many times and offered them his support in the event of a hybrid model being launched, though in vain. The prototypes are still ready in Biel for the series production. But Hayek has since moved away from the hybrid engine – he is now mainly concerned with fuel-cell technology.

To this purpose Hayek founded the Clean Power Group in autumn 2007. The mission of this company is to implement sustainable energy projects. The high-tech energy firm is no longer to concentrate solely on solutions for reducing noxious substance emissions from cars and households, but actually to make these entirely CO_2-free. To achieve the widest possible impact with his projects in the USA, too, Hayek brought the film star George Clooney onto the board of directors of the energy company. Clooney, who has long been campaigning for green projects in the USA, has the task of publicising the firm and its new products. This time, though, Hayek wants to avoid the mistakes he made with the Smart and he is proceeding more cautiously. Now he no longer wants to offer the car industry a finished vehicle, but to limit himself with the Clean Power Group to developing an eco-friendly propulsion system. Here the car industry has a lot of catching up to do.

MCC was not the only joint venture in another industry with which Hayek suffered a shipwreck. In the mid-1990s he joined with Siemens to set up Swatch Telecom AG. Here, again, he chose the wrong partner. As in the car industry, much bigger sums are involved than in the watch business. The plan was to manufacture small telecoms devices to generate a turnover of at least 200 million francs within three years. Siemens was to provide the technology for cordless phones and pagers, and SMH the skills in consumer goods marketing. The start was made by Siemens with a wireless phone in a Swatch design that was intended for the Italian market. Also planned was a multifunction pager that could store several access authorisations at the same time. Yet the collaboration between the two firms was short-lived. Just one year later, Siemens terminated the collaboration and sold its shares to SMH. However, Hayek's investment in this case was much smaller than at the time in the car project, being in the single millions. In any case, this effort at diversification also foundered. It turned out that the watch company could do little alone and without experts in the highly regulated telecoms market.

Hayek had already tried once before to gain a foothold in this market. The Twin-phone, a phone that enables more than two people to take part in a conversation at the same time, which had an eye-catching unconventional design, was also a failure. This phone was produced in Taiwan in several colour versions, and quality problems emerged very quickly. The device became a shelf-blocker not only in Switzerland but also in the USA. Hayek later made some highly self-critical comments about this venture as well, even referring to a strategic error. Hayek had to realise that he could not sell any phones in the Swatch stores without any collaboration from the telecoms companies. 'I did not understand at the time that money is not made from the phones themselves but by the owners paying to use the network of the telecoms companies.'

Hayek also had a less than lucky hand with the Swatch accessories. Mainly in the USA, Swatch tried to extend the watches product range with all kinds of gimmicks. From headbands to umbrellas and sunglasses, for a while almost anything could be bought in the Swatch stores. The turnover with these items was certainly enormous, but the revenues were rather unsatisfactory. The distribution and advertising costs came too heavily into the equation in this business. Hayek quickly put an end to the department store concept, not only because these experiments did not pay, but also because he was afraid they might weaken the Swatch brand. Generally, the Swatch Group has recently reduced its involvement in activities that add nothing to the core business.

10
The Contrarian Thinker – Hayek's Socio-political Standpoint

AYEK IS AN ORIGINAL thinker, and not only as an entrepreneur; he is also ever full of surprises with his comments on social and political issues. Whereas most of his fellow businessmen are in the middle-class political mainstream, Hayek cannot easily be classified with one ideological trend. He is not close to any political party, even the liberal FDP, although this remains the party with the most support in business circles. Hayek once said that he was disappointed by the Liberals, though without any clear explanation. Yet anyone who follows Hayek's opinions on political and social issues more closely quickly sees why he distances himself from the traditional party of business.

Hayek repeatedly clashed with important FDP figures in the past. When he exposed the spendthrift politicians in Bern with his report on the procurement of the Leopard 2 tank, some of the fiercest attacks on him came from the Liberals. Hayek had to realise that many parliamentarians are not too fastidious about the liberal principles of their party manifesto. The idea of competition and the demand for a frugal management of state finances are sometimes very freely interpreted by middle-class politicians according to where their interests lie and considerations of electoral tactics.

As an entrepreneur who relies primarily on market forces, Hayek does not of course get on all that well with the left. All the same, he has never refrained from entering alliances with the Social Democrats where necessary; for example, he did not hesitate to make contact with the SP President Helmut Hubacher over the Leopard tanks deal. Even when he later repeatedly adopted a strategic position on parliamentary matters, he never engaged intensively with Swiss politics. The full-blooded entrepreneur did not have the time. And anyway he would not have had the patience for any political office. The man of action is used to being able to implement his decisions immediately without having to protect himself in advance against all sides.

However, as a businessman Hayek could not operate in a total vacuum. He was repeatedly affected by political decisions in his business career, whether in the legal regulation of origin designations or the prohibition on night working for women. Through his commission for the Leopard survey, he got to know a large number of people who knew their way extremely well around the Bern parliamentary and administrative system. The Ringier journalist Frank A. Meyer used to be one of his 'antennae'. There was a time when Hayek was supposed to have phoned 'FAM', as Meyer is known in the media, almost every Saturday morning. As a long-standing federal parliamentary journalist and confidant of many Federal Councillors, he would have the latest information on internal matters in the Federal Council. Hayek is no longer dependent on Meyer's legendary network, but the contact over many years partly explains Hayek's good relations with *Blick*, *Sonntagsblick* and *Schweizer Illustrierte*. But this relationship was strained by an article that appeared in the financial weekly *Cash*, which described the Hayeks as 'Swiss royals, only without scandals'. From sheer anger, Hayek temporarily imposed an advertising boycott on the entire Ringier press.

Apart from this brief interlude, Hayek is still a well-liked regular visitor to the Ringier pages today. No other Swiss business leader's statements of opinion can be turned so neatly into snappy headlines. For instance, Hayek is the only notable Swiss businessman who has openly admitted to being an anti-militarist. Some of his views are even very close to the army abolitionists. 'Anything that reduces the army, leads it *ad absurdum*, is good', he once said to *Cash*. Only extremely left-wing Social Democrats would dare to express such heretical views in public today. Hayek often does not take the trouble to weigh up his words politically first. He is much too independent to let himself be monopolised politically by anyone. He can afford to be. He is his own lord and master and absolutely immune to pressure.

Hayek has also taken a highly critical stance on nuclear energy, although he once wanted to be a nuclear physicist. 'In the long term, nuclear energy is completely unacceptable', he said in 2003. Hayek was also one of the few businessmen who very early condemned extortionate managerial salaries – he did not hold back in his criticism, and this was long before it became a commendable everyday observation. Hayek considers it extremely perverse that a company share price often rises just after an announcement of redundancies. Many managers unnecessarily prescribe redundancies and thereby only prove their own incompetence. Generally they had simply misjudged the future prospects; that is, they had been over-optimistic and had therefore taken on too many staff. Hayek thinks long-term in recruitment policies. He knows that it makes little sense to put people out on the street and then only have to look for employees again as soon as the economy picks up again. Redundancies generally lead to a loss of valuable skills.

The managerial caste gets deservedly criticised in almost every other interview he gives. Hayek finds it unacceptable that many of these high-paid employees often do not even consider their job a full-time occupation and top up their salaries on the side with a series of appointments on boards of directors. He himself sits only on boards of directors in his own subsidiary companies. He has always consistently declined requests from other companies. He usually only accepts roles with a public dimension or a direct connection with his watch group. Thus the German Chancellor Helmut Kohl brought him onto his technology board in the mid-1990s as the only foreign consultant. Of course, Hayek has always cleverly used such appointments to create publicity for himself, his company and its products. He therefore does not want to spread himself too thin. For instance, Hayek never goes to the World Economic Forum (WEF) in Davos. 'Just as I don't go to church, I don't go to the World Economic Forum in Davos either', he once said. It is nothing but a 'forum of vanities'. Anyway, Hayek has not been on good terms with the WEF founder Klaus Schwab since he left the board of directors at the watch group.

Of course, it is not only the managers who attend Davos that Hayek criticises, but also always large numbers of entrepreneurs. They are usually not there on expenses, though, but at their own cost. In Hayek's view, these two kinds of company boss are worlds apart. He regards this as a very important distinction because he sees the credibility of entrepreneurs being put increasingly in jeopardy by the behaviour of irresponsible short-termist managers. Whereas entrepreneurs put their own money into the firm and therefore take risks, not much can actually happen to managers striving for the best possible stock market performance – apart from losing their job or bonus. For a long time, shareholders were not on their guard against the high-handedness of certain managers because they could also profit from rising share prices. However, Hayek has always been a fierce opponent of this shareholder-value thinking, a policy based primarily on shareholders' short-term interests. In his view, the company management has to take account of the concerns of all the stakeholders, which therefore includes the employees and the public. According to Hayek's conviction, it is the entrepreneur's core task to invest the profits generated in the firm's long-term development. The entrepreneur should create jobs or at least try to protect the existing ones.

Hayek sees Niklaus Schneider-Ammann as the embodiment of this type of entrepreneur. Hayek brought the engineering industrialist onto the board of directors at his Swatch Group some years ago. When the Biel machinery and plant contractor Mikron was on the verge of bankruptcy in 2003, the Langenthaler entrepreneur contributed his own money to the company reorganisation. As Chairman of the board of directors at Mikron, Schneider-Ammann felt partly responsible for this firm's difficulties and he did not want to walk away. The FDP National Councillor repeatedly championed the interests of Switzerland as a manufacturing base – he may not infrequently have been inspired here by Hayek, as he may also have been when – as was at least confirmed by some of his party colleagues – together with the watch magnate in 2007 he forked out around 100,000 francs for the security costs at the Swiss national celebrations on the Rütli. At the time, neither the Federal Government nor the Central Swiss cantons were willing to bear the security costs for the celebration speaker, Federal Councillor Micheline Calmy-Rey. Without Hayek's impetus, Schneider-Ammann would hardly have thought of it himself, according to those in his circle; unlike Hayek, he had never previously been someone who went in for speculative actions.

For Hayek, these activities with popular appeal are not a matter of his personal image but primarily a reassessment of the entrepreneur's public role. He wants to demonstrate that true entrepreneurs assume social responsibility. For this reason he also once suggested creating a Nobel Prize for entrepreneurs. The economics professors who until now have been honoured with the prestigious prize have in his view hardly ever deserved this honour. These scientists produce 'only theories, nothing concrete', he says. By making comments of this kind, Hayek quite often reveals a rather populistic hostility to academia.

For Hayek, it is not theoreticians but practitioners and entrepreneurs who create real value. The entrepreneur is an artist and money is the brush with which he constantly creates something new. Hayek certainly concedes that not every entrepreneur is an artist, but conversely he states that every artist is an entrepreneur. However, Hayek overlooks the important distinction that many of the great masters he admires lived on the breadline and were very bad businesspeople from a financial perspective.

There have been some exceptions, though: Pablo Picasso, for instance, was certainly not just a brilliant painter but also an entrepreneurially minded innovator and a marketing genius. Some of his pictures fetched among the highest prices at auction achieved by any living artist. Picasso is, in fact, the artist with whom Hayek constantly likes to compare himself – understatement is absolutely not one of the watch magnate's characteristics. 'Modesty is just hypocrisy in successful people', he says. Like the famous Spanish painter and sculptor, he says he also sees absolutely no reason to retreat from professional life just because of his advanced age.

When Hayek talks about the entrepreneur's work, he glows with enthusiasm. True entrepreneurs are selfless people, he once told the Zurich *Tages-Anzeiger* magazine. Altruism is something hardly anyone expects though from a company boss. Profit-seeking entrepreneurs fulfil a completely different role in society from figures such as Mother Teresa, who concerned herself with the poorest people in the Indian slums until her death. The business profession must not be idealised; it is enough if business leaders can fulfil their wider social responsibility. In this respect, many employee representatives actually pay tribute to the watch magnate. In the pursuit of his own interests, Hayek has so far also managed to enable employees to benefit from the success of the Swatch Group and indeed by providing relatively secure jobs. Hayek takes social partnership seriously. He has also made a substantial contribution to maintaining the economic fabric of the entire watchmaking region.

Hayek has certainly also had to make staff redundant. When he took over the management of the ASUAG/SSIH group, the reorganisation measures were not yet completed. Further adaptations had to be made that were painful for the employees. Yet Hayek never made his staff insecure with an unpredictable hire-and-fire policy. He also never imposed a brutal cost-cutting programme on the staff. He certainly behaved extremely brusquely and narrow-mindedly towards some people at the senior executive level, such as Ernst Thomke. Yet most of the ordinary employees were generally treated properly. Hayek is certainly a patriarch, but he realises that a good understanding with social partners is also in his own interests.

Hayek has an especially good, even warm relationship, with Christiane Brunner. From 1992 to 2000, she was General Secretary of the Swiss Metal- and Watch-workers' Union (SMUV). Their good relationship is all the more surprising given that Brunner's reputation as a trade unionist was for being highly combative. Yet the two socio-political opponents always showed each other mutual respect. Hayek was proud of his good relationship with Brunner, who only narrowly missed being elected to the Federal Council in 1993, and he also liked to show that in public. Brunner remembers an experience just before some negotiations were due to take place in the watch industry between the social partners in the mid-1990s. Hayek offered Brunner a lift in his Mercedes to the meeting at the Hotel Elite in Biel. The watch boss drove with the trade unionist not on any direct route but zigzagging through half of Biel; he stopped several times by the roadside, lowered the car window and asked passers-by the way to the Hotel Elite. Brunner could not understand Hayek's behaviour at first, since he must have known exactly where this town's famous hotel was. He had held his first press conference there after joining the ASUAG/SSIH group. But wherever Hayek stopped his car, both the watch industry VIPs were immediately recognised by people. Many of the passers-by they spoke to reacted with surprise. Hayek beamed about the whole thing every time it became obvious that the pedestrians to whom they spoke were baffled. Brunner began to realise that it was obviously pleasing Hayek when his good relationship with her was being registered by the public.

There is yet another event that Brunner can report that explains her good relations with the watch magnate. Western Swiss television wanted to make a documentary about the trade unionist. One of the scenes was to be filmed at the Lac de Joux, in the Waadtland Jura. Yet the weather was not helpful – a fierce storm was brewing in the Vallée de Joux. It was

Nicolas Hayek in 1992 with the trade union official Christiane Brunner. © Keystone.

summer and the holiday season. Certainly Hayek had broken very early on with the antiquated custom of so-called watchmaker holidays and introduced a continuous operation in his factories. He considered it an unreasonable demand that all the wheels should stop turning for weeks in the Jura while his customers waited for their goods. Nevertheless, the sparsely populated Jura valleys still look almost deserted in July and August today. Brunner knew that not much was happening in the nearby ETA factory at this time. She therefore suggested asking for permission to film there. The factory representative was stubborn and refused access to Brunner and the television crew. Brunner did not want to give in. She phoned the SMH group headquarters in Biel to ask if anything could be done. Hayek's secretary explained to her that the boss was away on a foreign trip. NGH – as Hayek is called inside the company – was on an aeroplane and so could not easily be contacted. But she would go and see whether anything could be arranged. Almost within the hour Brunner received a phone call from Hayek, who had since landed at a stopover point: 'Frau Brunner, that is no problem. I will immediately arrange for the gates to be opened for you at ETA.' Brunner has never forgotten Hayek's cooperation. Their good relationship had a positive influence on the relations between social partners across the whole watch industry. Brunner and Hayek often still put their heads together confidentially before official contract negotiations in the industry. What the two of them discussed in private often set the standard for the whole watch industry.

Once the entrepreneur and the union official even made common cause at the political level. After the millennium when the franc was growing ever stronger and the dollar rate was falling further and further, Hayek got nervous. The watch industry had already endured a bitter experience in the mid-1990s when watches became increasingly expensive in the foreign markets because of currency fluctuations. At that time, not only the watch industry but also the rest of the Swiss export industry was losing a lot of competitiveness. The strong franc gave Hayek a severe drop in margins and currency losses totalling 140 million francs. It was mainly the franc's relationships to the dollar that was causing problems for the watch industry. Nevertheless, the Swiss National Bank firmly refused to slow the rise in the franc by intervening in the currency markets. It feared that buying the dollar would expand the circulation of money in the Swiss national economy and therefore stoke inflation. Hayek lambasted Markus Lusser, President of the National Bank's board of directors, in many interviews for his bullish monetary policy. He was afraid that great damage was being done to the entire Swiss export economy. But, to his annoyance, Hayek received no support from Vorort, the economic umbrella organisation. The predecessor organisation of what is now Economiesuisse saw no reason whatsoever to act. And the NZZ, almost the liberal conscience of the Swiss economy, even criticised Hayek extremely harshly for his demand. Hayek knew nothing about monetary policy, wrote NZZ economics editor Gerhard Schwarz. And that was a generous interpretation. The negative interpretation was that Hayek was acting against superior knowledge from his own self-interest. As an entrepreneur, Hayek was isolated once again in the Swiss economy.

In 2002, a similar development occurred on the currency markets. This time the dollar still stood at around 1.30 francs, but again there were negative repercussions to be feared on jobs in the export economy. This time Hayek no longer wanted to wait for support from the trade associations. So he formed a kind of political duo with Christiane

Brunner, who was also concerned about jobs. As the SP President at that time, Brunner convinced her parliamentary party to submit a corresponding proposal in the National Council. This requested the Federal Council to undertake 'time-limited protective measures for the export industry against the collapse in the dollar'. For his part, in several interviews Hayek gave Brunner accompanying support in her effort to support the Swiss industrial zone. From a political viewpoint, their joint demand was rather naive, though, as the National Bank does not have to take orders from either the Federal Council or Parliament. But even recommendations would not have been necessary this time. The new management of the central bank spontaneously assured that it would struggle resolutely against any further revaluation of the franc. Even this signal had an impact.

Hayek never wanted to enter politics. His fame as one of the most successful businessmen meant that his voice was already being heard in that context. Hayek repeatedly complained that productive industry was inadequately represented under the cupola of the Federal Parliament building. Economiesuisse might well do some intensive lobbying in Bern, but Hayek had long held a poor view of this lobbying organisation. The economic umbrella association did not represent Switzerland's issues as a manufacturing base consistently enough. 'That's not the umbrella organisation for entrepreneurs; it's the umbrella association for managers', he once criticised. His companion Schneider-Ammann shared this critical view. As President of Swissmem, he even threatened a few years ago to pull his engineering industrialists' association out of Economiesuisse. Such a decision was also mooted within the watch industry at that time. As a driving force, Nicolas Hayek had very early brought the watch association Fédération Horlogère into line with corresponding financial pressure – his company is the largest contributor. The fact that Schneider-Ammann, a member of Swatch's board of directors, tried to take a similar line with Economiesuisse suggests that he may have discussed this matter with Hayek.

The economic umbrella association Economiesuisse has always had something of a reputation for acting primarily in the interests of the pharmaceutical industry and the banks and neglecting the issues of the other industries, especially industrial small and medium-sized enterprises (SMEs). Since a change of management in the association, however, Hayek has changed his view. In 2008 the economic umbrella organisation even invited him to give a speech at the annual meeting. On the 'day of the economy' Hayek was full of praise: 'With its efficient board of directors under Gerold Bührer's truly Swiss and entrepreneurial leadership, Economiesuisse is revealing a clear, combative spirit.' What had specifically caused his change of opinion, he did not say.

However, Hayek's critical attitude to politics and administration has not changed. When China raised import duty on Swiss watches to protect its own industry, Bern only reacted very timidly. Hayek was convinced that if something similar had happened with the banks, the nation would have been climbing onto the barricades. And the financial centre even managed to obtain a parliamentary discussion of writing banking secrecy into the Federal Constitution. 'If foreign politicians question banking secrecy, then we will all immediately be ready for battle, including the Federal Council.'

The banks always get very short shrift from Hayek anyway. This can be explained by Hayek's experiences with the financial sector as an entrepreneur. When the watch companies SSIH and ASUAG were getting into difficulty, he came to realise as a consultant that despite their great influence in the watch industry the financial institutions lacked the necessary knowledge of the sector. At that time, for two pins the Swiss Bank Corporation and the Union Bank would have sold off the Omega brand to the Japanese. If Hayek had not urgently advised against it, this would have spelt the end for the core of the Swiss watch industry. To Hayek, the financial centre has far too much power in the Swiss real economy. This is also one of the key reasons why many highly traditional firms such as Sulzer or Bally are only now a fraction of their former size.

There are some other reasons, though, for Hayek's discontent. The watch industrialist has always felt unfairly treated by the banks' financial analysts. In 1997 he suspected various institutions of having artificially suppressed the Swatch share price. Since such an act had just become punishable under Swiss law, Hayek was the first to seek to take legal proceedings in this matter, including against Goldmann Sachs and the Bank Corporation. It annoyed Hayek that his company share price did not budge an inch, while almost all the other listed companies could profit from the stock market boom. The Zurich district attorney, however, suspended the proceedings after a short period since the requisite criteria were not met for such a complaint.

That was not the last time that Hayek acted against financial institutions. When, early in 2008, just before the Swatch Group annual press conference, the Zurich Cantonal Bank advised its customers to exchange the watch group stock for Procter & Gamble shares, the watch magnate was furious. He and his son Nick cancelled the traditional meeting with the bank analysts that took place annually after the press conference. They disinvited the whole pack of them at short notice. Moreover, with an advert entitled 'Is the ZKB deceiving its customers again?', the father and son tried to vent their anger in a large public sphere as well. Yet most of the newspapers refused to carry the advert on legal grounds.

The property bubble that burst in the USA in 2008 and the ensuing global stock market decline confirmed Hayek's view that something was amiss in the financial markets and that there was an urgent need for action. This crisis showed that inadequate control of finance was not a national but an international problem. Monitoring must therefore be tackled by multilateral means, Hayek argued. In the Swatch Group's 2007 annual report, his presidential foreword called for 'massive reforms' that would have to target a 'better control of the international financial market system'. Unlike his namesake, the Austrian economist Friedrich August von Hayek who died in the early 1990s, Nicolas Hayek is anything but a market fundamentalist. He does not oppose every form of state intervention in the economy. He even calls for regulations 'to limit the acquisition of large shareholdings to investors who are familiar with the culture, the products and the goals of the company concerned'. How this should be done, though, Hayek does not say. Meeting this demand would almost amount to a suitability test for investors, which would hardly be realistic. For Hayek, the point is merely that the real economy should not continue to be bossed around by the monetary economy, because in his view it is primarily industry that creates prosperity. This he terms the 'value-making' economy, in contrast to the financial sector which he regards as the 'value-taking' economy.

Such unqualified statements cause irritation. Hayek often says what he thinks thoughtlessly and directly. He also prefers people who speak plainly and are comprehensible to him. Whether someone is on the left or right politically is less important to him. So, for instance, he occasionally also found words of praise for Christoph Blocher, the leading figure in the Swiss People's Party (SVP). Blocher's isolationist European policy is certainly anathema to Hayek. He also has no time for his management principle that places the contract above the person. In Hayek's view, the businessman has to fulfil consumer needs rather than an abstract contract or even a mission, as propagated by Blocher. However, Hayek's national pride is as strong and emotional as Blocher's. When Switzerland was criticised in certain circles in the USA for having unlawfully kept the funds of Holocaust victims during the Second World War, Hayek sided with the SVP politician. He also criticised the media and the Swiss politicians for being mealy-mouthed and insufficiently on their guard. Hayek called the discussion about the Holocaust funds a 'hypocrisy of collective guilt'. At his Swatch boutique in New York, he even ostentatiously flew two Swiss flags and enlarged the lettering 'Swiss'. He thereby consciously took the risk of falling by the wayside commercially in this market.

It is Blocher's uncompromising political style that impresses Hayek. That is why at the time he welcomed the SVP politician's election to the Federal Council and later regretted his being voted out. Hayek essentially supported Blocher's restrictive asylum policy as well, though with one important difference. Unlike Blocher, Hayek is convinced that if the industrial countries want to slow the influx of asylum-seekers, they should contribute more to the economic development of the southern countries as a countermeasure, to eliminate the grounds for fleeing from poverty.

It is not only his unconventional opinions that make it impossible to classify Hayek politically. He is also difficult to understand because he often changes his position over the course of time. Once a fervent supporter of Switzerland's entry to the EU, he has since become a fierce critic of the European Union. Switzerland must join the EU and 'as fast as possible or we will soon only be producing milk and cheese', he said in 1991 just before the European Economic Area (EEA) referendum. Certainly Hayek still calls himself a convinced European today. As indeed he must be: Hayek gains almost half his turnover in Europe. For him, there is only any question of Switzerland joining if the EU were to become more democratic. He complains that Brussels today is constantly making new laws that create difficulties for the economy.

On the question of origin designations, though, it is Hayek who is calling for stricter laws. He would like the 'Swiss-made' criteria to be tightened. The EU refuses. According to current regulations, a watch can be labelled 'Swiss-made' if only half its components come from Switzerland. This determination corresponds to the watch treaty agreed between Switzerland and the EU in 1972. Hayek and other large Swiss watch manufacturers take the view that at least 80 per cent of the parts in a mechanical watch and at least 60 per cent in an electronic watch should be domestically produced. If the industry does not manage in this way to be better distinguished from the Asian competition, Hayek considers that the existence of the Swiss watch industry will be endangered in the medium term. Conversely, European suppliers of the watch industry must fear that if the origin designation criteria were made stricter, they would lose contracts from Switzerland.

However, Hayek takes a much more critical attitude to the USA than to the EU. As the citizen of a small state, he always disliked the careless superpower politics of George W. Bush's administration. The way the USA has always exercised its role as a protective power towards Israel in particular may be a factor for Hayek because of his Lebanese origins.

Hayek considers that many questionable developments have spilled over into Europe from the other side of the Atlantic since the Second World War. The short-term drive for profit that also began to catch on in Switzerland in the early 1990s is to Hayek the prime cause of many undesirable economic developments. Long before the collapse of the American banking system, Hayek warned about this possibility. The USA is certainly a giant in military terms, but economically it has a much weaker constitution than is believed, Hayek explained to the German *Manager Magazin* years before the financial crisis. At the boardroom level of most other Swiss companies, though, it is only the devastating repercussions of the crisis that have brought a reversal of opinion. Previously it was common to adopt uncritically all the financial fashionable trends that came from the USA. The dynamism and success of the American economic model was also used to justify excessive managerial salaries.

This critical attitude towards the USA, though, is hardly the reason why Hayek has relatively rarely visited this country. With a turnover share of under 10 per cent, he is in fact much less dependent on the American market than many of his competitors. Furthermore, Hayek does not particularly like travelling in general. The marketing genius visits the markets surprisingly little. He feels cramped and not

especially well in aeroplanes. A few unpleasant experiences may also
have contributed to this. In 1989 an unsettling flight experience in
Hong Kong left him shaking. At that time aeroplanes still landed at
the old airport Kai Tak in the middle of the skyscrapers. For pilots, the
extremely short runway at the airport that was decommissioned ten
years later was a real challenge because it ended just at the water's edge.
This extremely difficult landing manoeuvre often resulted in aeroplanes
being driven off the middle of the runway by blasting side-winds. So
this time, too, the pilot had to go round again at the last moment in
his first attempt to land. As Eric Steiner, who was then responsible for
the Rado brand in China, recalls, Hayek described this incident to him
at the dinner afterwards as a truly horrific experience.

In Hayek's few journeys to the USA, his media appearances, such
as in 1996 at the Atlanta Olympics, always had an especially strong,
broad appeal. There Hayek was allowed to carry the Olympic torch
as the only business representative. At that time it was the Swatch
that appeared as the timekeeper for Hayek's company. It took a great
deal to persuade him to make this journey, according to colleagues in
his circle at the time. When he arrived in the Southern USA, Hayek
may have almost slightly regretted giving into this – it was 37 degrees
centigrade. So Hayek covered the 500-metre running track at a snail's
pace, taking a full ten minutes. Here Marianne's encouraging shouts
did not help much, as she stood in a T-shirt printed with a picture of
her husband at the roadside. However, Hayek did not want his leisurely
pace to be explained by any deficient condition. As in most situations,
here, too, he had an answer ready, claiming to one journalist: 'I wanted
to make the most of the incredible atmosphere at the torch relay. And
that only works if you take it at a comfortable pace.'

One year earlier with Concorde, Hayek took things in a much less
leisurely way than in Atlanta. What was then the fastest aeroplane in
the world carried him at supersonic speed across the Atlantic. This
time, too, there was an unusual reason for the journey. Hayek had
received the unique opportunity to present his Chronos UNlimited at
the 50th anniversary of the United Nations (UN), a genuine first. Never
before had a businessman been allowed to advertise his products at the
UN headquarters. At this opportunity Hayek even achieved the feat
of identifying common features between his company objectives and
those of the international organisation. He said that just as the UN was

Nicolas and Marianne Hayek at the Atlanta Olympics in 1996.

not a purely idealistic organisation, the SMH was not guided only by material goals. He also immediately tried to prove it with his actions by promising to put five francs into a fund for youth education projects for every watch sold. The effect of his appearance was correspondingly great. The magazine *Forbes*, the TV broadcaster CNN and many other well-known international media interviewed the clever businessman and gave him a platform to spread his advertising message worldwide.

When the UN Secretary-General, Kofi Annan, asked Hayek and a few other billionaires such as Ted Turner and Bill Gates each to contribute $1 billion to a charitable fund, however, Hayek firmly refused. For him, this request went too far. What the UN lacked was not primarily money. Instead, the international organisation needed more respect from the member countries, Hayek told the French daily newspaper *Le Monde*, with reference to the US intervention in Iraq. Unlike the US investor Warren Buffett and the Microsoft founder Bill Gates, Hayek has no intention of putting his billions of capital into a foundation and bequeathing it to the general public. Instead, he wants to be able to pass on his life's work some day to his family.

Nicolas Hayek and his son Nick present a Swatch Chronos UNlimited to the
UN Secretary-General Boutros-Ghali at the 50th anniversary of the UN in 1995.

Hayek's repeated promotion of the UN's goals may not be dismissed
out of hand, though, as a propaganda stunt in his own cause. Even in
his youth in Lebanon, Hayek was sensitised to the world organisation's
battle in the field of human rights by his uncle Charles Malik. Hayek is
by no means indifferent to social injustices. I was reminded of this in
a conversation following an interview that I conducted with him some
years ago. Hayek told me at the time about a visit by the Richemont
President Johann Ruport to his daughter Nayla's stud farm. On this
occasion the South African pointed in amusement at the electric fence
that surrounded the horses' field. 'We also needed fences like that in
those days to keep the blacks away from our houses', said the boss of
the luxury watch brands Cartier, Mont Blanc and IWC. Hayek was
deeply shocked by this cynical remark.

I will also never forget an experience in Hayek junior's office. It
was 11 September 2001. I had just asked Nick Hayek what the black
flag with the skull and crossbones on his office window signified. Like
pirates in the past, he had always been a rebel, he replied. Swatch
embodied this rebellious and revolutionary spirit. Suddenly, in the

middle of our conversation, the secretary stormed into the office and told us about the attack on the Twin Towers in New York. Shortly afterwards, Hayek senior also came in. Together we followed on the television in consternation as the two towers in Manhattan collapsed. 'That was bound to happen one day', was the gist, quoted from memory, of Hayek's short comment. Hayek is convinced that the prime causes of terrorism lie in the social and political conditions of the southern hemisphere countries. In his view, fanaticism cannot be combated by repression alone. In this judgement, too, Hayek diverged from the emerging view at the time during the Bush administration of a battle between cultures.

11

The Family Express – Hayek's Plans for his Company's Future

AYEK HAS A VERY strong sense of family. He once said that he was too volatile to be a good father. Yet that does nothing to detract from the family's importance to him. Hayek spends most of his private life among his family, away from parties and VIP functions. As in his company, Hayek also sets the tone at home, as his wife Marianne has already occasionally revealed in interviews. He has certainly always given his daughter Nayla, his son Nick and his grandson Marc a free rein. He has made his children gain experience in completely different professions. It is no coincidence, though, that today all three offspring hold leading positions in the Swatch Group.

Hayek's main concern is that the company should continue to be run in line with his views after his death. He therefore wants to pass on his life's work to his descendants. Not all company founders have such great confidence in their children and grandchildren. It is not unusual for successful family businesses to be ruined by the heirs after the founder retires. This observation was made by the first Chancellor of the German Empire, Otto von Bismarck: 'The first generation creates wealth, the second generation administers wealth, the third generation studies art history and the fourth generation goes completely degenerate', he is supposed to have said.

If Bismarck's theory were right, Hayek's company would be in bad shape. For several years, his son Nick has already been successfully running the Swatch Group. The excellent results achieved by the company since the change of generations seems to contradict Bismarck's pessimistic view. As the representative of the second generation, Nick has so far shown himself to be much more than an administrator. The son still has his father and mentor behind him, though. Hayek makes no secret of the fact that he still largely holds the reins: 'But of course I steer the course that we are taking', he said to *Welt online* in 2008, a few months after his 80th birthday. No one should be deceived about this fact simply because the old man has stopped appearing at annual results presentations in the last few years. Nicolas Hayek still exercises his mandate as President and delegate of the board of directors very actively. Father and son are in constant contact. One of their acquaintances reports that in a conversation he had with Nick in his office they were interrupted around three times in two hours by phone calls from his father.

Nicolas Hayek is as energetic and omnipresent as ever. 'I don't work, I have fun', says Hayek. He still drives almost every day to the head office in Biel or to one of his many offices in the various subsidiary companies. He often works late into the night, say employees at the watch group. Whereas other businessmen have long since retired at his age or at least moved down a gear, Hayek works as if life will never end. It is totally convincing when he says he still very much enjoys it. Hayek certainly struggles with his weight, but he has almost never been ill. He is on his feet at six o'clock in the morning. 'He stays even when he has reached the sell-by date', head-hunter Sandro Gianella said about Hayek even in the mid-1990s. He obviously did not mean it pejoratively. He only meant that a successful, full-blooded entrepreneur cannot just be pushed aside, as Gianella comments with hindsight on his remark.

Succession arrangements present a problem for many family businesses. One third of the 500 biggest Swiss firms are family-owned. In the ideal scenario, the descendant who is a designated successor earns his spurs first in another company. When he has built up some achievements there, he is brought by his father into the family business and then he grows into his new task. Usually, however, the succession does not follow the textbook. Many ageing company owners experience great difficulty letting go and keep postponing the decision. Even successful business leaders such as the Mövenpick founder Uli Prager, or Rudolf Sprüngli, the former boss of the chocolate company Lindt & Sprüngli, have failed in this regard.

With Nicolas Hayek, too, it looked for a long time as if he could not decide. At times the Swatch share price came under pressure not least because of the uncertainty surrounding the company's future. When Hayek was asked about his succession, he constantly put off the question. If he were run over by a car, he always replied, there were enough capable people in the company who could take over the management. However, many insiders placed a big question mark over this assertion, for the Swatch Group had been a complete one-man show since Ernst Thomke's departure. Certainly, there were some competent senior staff in the group management apart from Nicolas Hayek. Yet Hayek's autocratic management style hardly allowed any of these senior executives to gain a profile. Hayek always took almost all the important decisions himself.

It was only when he had already passed beyond retirement age that his intentions gradually became clear. Hayek brought his son Nick into the company and gradually built him up as his successor. At first this caused great scepticism in the investing public, for Nick did not have any relevant track record at this point. He was a totally blank slate. Apart from a short work placement in a foundry in Wintherthur, he had never had any experience in another company. Almost no one but the company boss trusted the scion to run a billion-franc company.

Certainly Nick had to make a modest start. At results presentations he was initially seen laying out the cables for the slide-show to present the latest products. Among other things, he also concerned himself with the Swatch advertising. Nick had been very creative, Marianne Egli remembers, who was then responsible for Swatch PR. He had put his hand to the wheel whenever necessary. The top boss's son soon moved fast through the company hierarchy in great strides. In 1995, he was suddenly appointed Marketing Director of Swatch. In ten years, he was already the tenth person to hold this post. Hayek explained the promotion as follows:

> A year ago the senior executives came to me and said I absolutely must ensure that my son Nick, who was already working part-time for Swatch as a commercials and advertising assistant, came completely into the firm. I told them to go away because for one thing he does not want that himself and secondly he told me that a son should prove without his father that he is better. Then the whole group management put me under pressure, saying I could not act against the company's interests.

But hardly anyone believed that the impetus for this promotion came not from Hayek but from the staff – less still that the old man had let himself be pressurised. The reason for Nick's speedy rise was entirely different. Completely unexpectedly, Hayek had to replace Franco Bosisio, who was involved in a bribery scandal in Italy.

However, sceptical voices inside the company that saw Nick only as the company boss's son soon fell silent. It was also possible to see the future more clearly. At least it was certain that the son was designated as a successor and was definitely supposed to be following in his father's footsteps. In 2000, Nick was chosen as Chief Executive by the seven-strong board of directors. This was moving a bit too fast for Nick, though. He did not yet feel ready to take on this great responsibility. It is said that he suggested to the board of directors that his father should continue to exercise this role for a while longer. Just three years later he was then finally appointed CEO of the whole group as crown prince of the Hayek dynasty. The only remaining question was whether Nick would also in fact be equal to this task.

Not only as an employee, but also as a boss, he quickly gained recognition in the company. He never played on being the owner's son, say people who worked closely with him. Outside the Swatch Group, however, especially among journalists and bank analysts, Nick was still not taken really seriously. A few trivial external things may certainly also have contributed to the impression of some observers that they were dealing with a kind of 'bonsai Hayek', a pocket edition of the father. Nick is just as fond of expensive cigars as his father. The old man has since given up smoking cigars, though, on his dentist's advice. Nick also acquired the habit of wearing several watches on his wrist at the same time. Like his father, he has a strong nose and bushy eyebrows. Both seem to want to disprove the saying that 'clothes make the person'. Father and son both hate ties. Nick, in fact, goes round in even more informal clothes than his father, often in jeans and rolled-up jacket sleeves, as was fashionable in the 1990s. The manager's dress code means nothing to him.

The fact that this lively young man will keep the largest watch company in the world on a successful course in future was initially unthinkable to many outside observers. Yet the company boss Nicolas Hayek already had great plans for his son Nick at an early stage. He sent Nick, whose full name is the same as his grandfather's, Georges Nicolas, to the Montana private school on the Zugerberg at a young age. There he could concentrate on preparing for his final school exams in the isolated boarding school environment. His father then sent him to St Gallen University, where students hoping for high honours often lay the foundations of their business careers. Yet Nick could not summon much enthusiasm for the dry theories taught there. In St Gallen he was often seen zooming up and down the Rosenberg in his Lamborghini. He gave up his studies after just four terms, to his father's disappointment. Yet he accepted the decision. Hayek is very understanding towards his own family, although he is felt by his subordinates in his company to be a patriarch, and he himself had been brought up in Lebanon according to very conservative principles.

In any case, Hayek has only limited regard for academic education. He funded Nick at his request for training at the film academy in Paris. The move from the management mill in the eastern Swiss province to the big-city environment of Parisian Bohemia was a leap into a completely different world for him. This was also expressed in his lifestyle. Nick traded in his luxury limo for a Fiat Panda. After completing these studies, he made two or three films. None of these films became a box-office hit. However, for one of these films, in which Peter Fonda appears, Nick received first prize at the Charlie Chaplin Comedy Film Festival in Vevey. The film was significantly entitled *Family Express*. Soon afterwards, the young filmmaker was actually to pursue an express career as a Hayek family member.

Like his father, Nick has not changed his lifestyle much with his ascent to the heights of the watch empire. He avoids jetset parties. Unlike his father, Nick consistently protects his private life from the public. There are no home-based features about him. He lives on the Zürichberg with his wife Liliana from Sarajevo. Nick is also known to be a passionate helicopter pilot. His pilot's licence not only enables him to fly to Finland in the holidays but also gives him great mobility at work. By helicopter Nick can reach his European subsidiaries in a flash. This mode of transport entirely suits his character: 'With the heli I can not only fly both forwards and backwards, but also hover very low over the landscape and so stay close to people', he said recently in a radio interview. When he is asked about his expensive hobby, Nick reacts with some embarrassment. As the son of rich parents, he was always very spoilt. At St Gallen University and especially at the film academy in Paris, he was much better off financially than most of his fellow students. Nick never flaunted his money, though. At the military training school, he never behaved at all like a son with a famous father, says a former fellow-soldier. They sensed instead that he found it painful appearing to have a special position. But most of the soldiers in his company knew that Nick always parked his luxury car well hidden in the neighbouring village when he returned from leave. 'For us, though, he was still an ordinary soldier like all the rest', says a former colleague with whom he completed his military training.

For Nick, the weeks in green uniform were not a happy time. His deep dislike of the army stems not only from his education but also from the military training school. Like his father, he takes the view that blind obedience and extremely hierarchical thinking stifle creativity and motivation. In the 1970s, when he was completing his military training, the army was still infused by Prussian discipline. So there was never any question of Nick completing officer training. As a flight observer he preferred to go off into the bushes to talk with a few fellow-soldiers in training about Dadaism or interesting books. As CEO of his billion-franc company, Nick is still an unconventional person. He can occasionally make statements that completely baffle the public, for instance when he was interviewed by Radio DRS 3 with Omega as the official timekeeper at the Olympic Games in Beijing. He said he felt much more at home in China than in the USA. Many bad developments came from the USA, as the subprime crisis showed. In China he found that people had a much less selfish attitude. When asked if he had not also observed negative developments in the Middle Kingdom, Hayek junior replied that these problematic aspects were mainly a legacy of the colonialism that the country had suffered. Nick revealed himself, probably to the amazement of many listeners, as a great admirer of the People's Republic of China under Communist Party rule. And this was at a time when Tibetan independence was a major topic in the media in Europe.

However, the CEO of the Swatch Group is not quite the rebel that he likes to imagine. As a businessman in any case he must be guided entirely by the needs and tastes of his customers. Anyone who does not 'adapt' in the market fails as a businessman. Even in his youth, Nick lacked the opposition and authorities against which he might have been able to chafe. Through his background, Nick met open doors almost everywhere. The black skull-and-crossbones flag that he has had hanging on his office window in Biel for years as a sign of his 'rebelliousness' is more of a playful gesture. Nick loves unconventional things. He is an admirer of Dadaism. He has always been fascinated by the movement that attracted discussion at the beginning of the twentieth century for its rejection of conventional literary and artistic forms. As a tribute to this intellectual movement, he once had a Dada watch specially made. Nick performed a PR stunt in 2002 at the Basel watch fair by proclaiming a 27th canton, the 'Swatch canton'. Citizenship should be awarded there to all those people who enjoy life like the wearers of the Swatch. The Cantonal Bank there should issue time instead of notes and coins. And there would be no taxes. Such dashes of colour that both Nick and his father try to bring into the otherwise rather dry business news are, of course, usually happily picked up by the media.

Not all the newspapers always made themselves available though for disseminating that kind of soft news, especially not the serious-minded NZZ. The Swatch Group boss has a deep aversion to this publication that still enjoys the highest credibility in Swiss business circles. 'I cannot even touch this paper', he said once. He does, however, like to read the left-wing French daily newspaper *Libération*, which does not usually treat businesspeople with kid gloves. Nick hates rigid intellectual schemas. He has inherited and learnt from his father the curiosity always to consider rules and conventions in a critical way. Actually, Nick is not afraid of being exposed by asking supposedly stupid questions, even at press conferences, when he is in the limelight. As a boss, Nick does not claim to know everything about his company. He says that asking questions is the only way to learn anything new. The Swatch Group CEO admits that, unlike his father, he does not have a head for figures. He prefers having the company figures explained by able employees to having to analyse and interpret them himself. Hayek's son prefers to go to a brainstorming session in preparation for a marketing event than to a budget meeting.

He is anything but a penny-pincher. Yet occasionally father and son can also switch roles in financial matters. So, for example, at the time Nicolas Hayek wanted to set the price of the ultra-thin Skin Swatch much lower than Nick. Yet Nick finally prevailed.

As CEO and Vice-President, Nick is now firmly in the saddle at the Swatch Group. After him it is highly probable that Nicolas Hayek's grandson, Marc Alexander, today boss of the Blancpain brand, will take over the helm. Marc has already made that clear in an interview. When he was asked a few years ago by the western Swiss financial magazine *Bilan* about a possible succession as a representative of the third generation, he replied: 'That is true. I assure you, though, that I never give it any thought. Certainly, it is important that the management of the group stays in the family but I really have a lot of time left before Nick's departure to get used to my responsibility.' So it is fairly clear even today that Marc will be Hayek III in future in the family dynasty.

Marc is the son of Nicolas Hayek's daughter Nayla. When he was born in 1971, Nayla was only 19 years old. Only shortly after her marriage to the Aargau businessman Roland Weber, Nayla got divorced. So Marc was brought up by his grandparents from the age of three and grew up well cared for at Lake Hallwil. Marc calls his grandmother Mam and his biological mother Nayla. Like Nick, almost all possibilities are open to him. The grandparents had a BMX track built for their grandchild behind the house so that he could train on his bike. When he was twelve years old, and Marc took his grandparents' name, he already greatly honoured his family by becoming a Swiss champion in his cycling discipline. Yet that did not satisfy Marc. He traded in the light bicycle for a heavy motorbike and also successfully contested many competitions in this sporting field. Marianne Hayek drove her grandson halfway around Switzerland so that he could take part in various motorbike races. This hobby also brought Marc into contact with the watch industry. As a member of the Certina racing team, he competed in international races on his 750 cc superbike over a long period. He helped to publicise the Certina brand among consumers. At the same time Marc busied himself with sponsoring this middle-price segment brand of the watch company.

Marc had gained some theoretical knowledge of marketing in Los Angeles. Like Nick, however, he broke off his studies early, and then gained some practical experience in this field as an employee at the Swatch Collectors Club. Yet Marc did not stay at Swatch for long. He was drawn to gastronomy. He had inherited his biological father's passion for wines. With a diploma in oenology in his pocket, he established a club-like bar called The Colors in Zurich when he was 27 years old. It was in the best city-centre location, on the ground floor of the Hayek Engineering building in the rooms where Uli Prager had then opened his first Mövenpick restaurant. So Marc remained in close contact with his family. At this time he lived with Nick, his uncle and 'brother' in a flat on the Zürichberg.

However, Hayek very soon brought his grandson into his company, and indeed with 'gentle pressure', as it was then called in the Swatch Group. He gave him a position as a marketing specialist at Blancpain alongside one of his most successful employees, Jean-Claude Biver, who had once revived this slumbering brand and brought it into the Swatch Group. The fact that Hayek was bringing one family member after another into a position in his company soon made it clear to everyone that this would also not be the final stopping point for Marc. Biver must also have realised this. In any case he quickly drew his own conclusions and left the group management of the Swatch Group. He found a new challenge at the Hublot brand. Marc took over full responsibility for Blancpain in 2002. However, unlike many other former managers of the Swatch Group, Biver never held his cold removal from power against Hayek. Today he is still full of praise for his former mentor, although he would have had ample cause to feel aggrieved, for today the success of the brand in the company is attributed almost exclusively to Marc. Since he took over the management of Blancpain, Hayek once said, the brand was growing very strongly. That is, in fact, correct. Yet it was Biver who created the conditions that enabled Marc to build on a firm foundation.

Marc lives with his wife of Cuban origin in western Switzerland. Today, he is also responsible for Frédéric Piguet. This factory has great strategic value in the group, since it provides the prestige brand of the Swatch Group with high-quality mechanical movements. As a member of the inner group management of the Swatch Group, Marc is also now responsible for the Middle East and Central America. Including him, there are now three generations of the Hayek family at the helm of the company.

Yet Nicolas, Nick and Marc Hayek are not the only family members at the top of the company. Even in 1995 Hayek had brought his daughter Nayla onto the board of directors. Since the beginning of 2008, she has also managed the Tiffany watch brand, which emerged from an alliance with the American jewellery company of the same name. Nayla has been able to build a strong network through her horse-breeding in the Arab world and has excellent connections with the royal houses there. In Saudi Arabia, though, she cannot use these very much because women have no place there in the business world. It is different in the Gulf States. Nayla is away there for several months a year as a consultant. She spends much of this time working at the Swatch Group head office in Dubai. Her knowledge of Arabic among other things has proved useful there.

Nayla actually wanted to study archaeology after her final school exams. But then her hobby, horse breeding, gradually became her profession. It all began with a pony that she received as a present from her parents as a young girl. When Nayla grew older, a few Irish jumpers and an Anglo-Arab mare were added. At that time Nayla still believed her mare was a proper Arab horse. Yet when the Crown Prince Faisal of Saudi Arabia was once visiting the Hayeks, he enlightened the young woman. So that she would finally get to know this noble horse breed properly, the crown prince gave her a thoroughbred Arab mare. The horse, called Ayesha, did not take very well to the journey, but soon the mare produced a foal. This was Nayla's opportunity to enter the world of horse breeding properly. So she later gained the possibility of getting her revenge on the Saudi royal house. In 1992 she gave up her grey horse Omega-Massud so that the German Finance Minister Jürgen Möllemann could give the valuable horse to King Fahd on his state visit. Nayla killed two birds with one stone, since the horse named after the prestige brand was, after all, the best advertising for Omega in the desert country.

Nayla Hayek very quickly made a name for herself in horse breeding. On the Lägern, a foothill of the Juras near Baden, she owns an idyllically situated stud farm with the Arabic name 'Hanaya', meaning 'little joy'. In a place surrounded by hedges and woods, Nayla keeps several dozen horses, mainly Arab thoroughbreds. Originally it was a farm that was shown as a model farm at the Swiss National Exhibition in 1964. At the end of the Expo it was dismantled and rebuilt on the Lägern.

So, in future, a horse breeder, a former film director and a former bar manager will determine the fate of the world's largest watch manufacturer. Hayek senior is certainly still bursting with energy, although he is already over 80 years old today. But he may not easily be able to stand at his descendants' sides for very much longer. At first sight this recruitment policy looks very much like family corruption or even nepotism. Actually, it might be thought that abilities and suitability rather than blood relationships should be critical in the selection process at the top of such an important company.

What is known as 'Buddenbrooks syndrome',* lack of innovation, has already led many companies into the abyss. Where it is almost only family members who still take on the most important positions in a large company, the available skills become distinctly limited. 'It's like assembling the Olympic team for 2020 from the eldest sons of the gold medal winners from the year 2000', as the famous US investor Warren Buffett once said.

Yet Hayek takes a different view. For him, neither diplomas nor achievement records in other professional fields are foremost considerations in planning his succession. He regards the emotional bond with the company as much more important with a consumer product like the watch. This emotional involvement has the most impact in connection with the operational responsibility taken by his offspring. That Hayek himself has so far given his company a face is actually an important part of his formula for success. This identity should be maintained by the long-term connection between the firm and the Hayek family. 'Because we all put our hearts into working at this company, no one thinks of selling shares in order maybe to run away and build a beautiful life on a desert island', argues Hayek.

After the mistakes that have brought many managers in public companies under criticism, family businesses are enjoying greater public confidence again. A study conducted by the Lausanne Management Institute IMD a few years ago in stock exchange-listed family companies also revealed that these achieved better results over a ten-year period than firms with widely dispersed shareholders. The director of the study, Professor Joachim Schwass, explains this by saying that family companies pursue a policy based on longer-term considerations. They rely less often on external consultants. The person who invests his own money usually exercises more caution.

For Hayek it would be a horrific scenario if his company one day became a football of hedge funds or other anonymous investors. Hayek regards the stock exchange as a casino, a playing field for speculators who gain vast sums on the back of small investors. He therefore constantly strove to establish personal control over the Swatch Group step by step. Even from the mid-1990s, Hayek began

---

* *Translator's note: Buddenbrooks* is a novel by Thomas Mann published in 1901 that charts the decline of a prosperous mercantile family in Lübeck over four generations.

to launch one share-buyback scheme after another. The purchased securities were destroyed each time, which reduced the share capital and drove up Hayek's stake accordingly. At general meetings, criticisms were therefore repeatedly made by the shareholders that this money would be better spent on higher dividends. Yet Hayek does not let such objections deter him. His family and institutions and people close to him now already comprise 41 per cent of the share capital. As soon as Hayek reaches the 49 per cent threshold, he must, according to the statutes, submit a takeover bid to the remaining investors. But statutes can be changed by a majority decision. For him as the main shareholder, that would probably be relatively easy. Should Hayek actually remove his company from the stock exchange list, the Swatch Group would become a pure family business.

If he could afford to do it now, Hayek would dearly love to turn his back on the stock exchange. Yet that would be too big an undertaking even for him. Depending on the stock exchange situation, to 'go private' he would need up to 10 billion francs more. A bid to shareholders would also drive up the share price and therefore the amount that Hayek would have to pay. The successful businessman would certainly have no trouble getting a bank loan to increase his stake. But that is not in question for Hayek. He would in future have to deal not only with uncomfortable, know-all analysts but probably at best with direct interference attempts by his creditors in the running of his company. Hayek prefers to build on his family, with whom he is convinced he has the guarantee of maintaining the previous share price.

Through the owners' emotional connections with their firms, family businesses hold some serious trump cards over anonymous public companies. The model only works, though, as long as all family members adhere to the predetermined shared system of values and goals. In Swiss business history there are also examples of the goals and interests of family members diverging after the founder's demise, with the firm having to suffer under quarrels between its owners. Today, Hayek senior, as a charismatic figurehead, provides the guarantee that everyone is pulling together. Whether his descendants will succeed in following in these big footsteps, only time will tell.

12

Hayek's Balance Sheet – a Watch Emporium on a Firm Foundation

NICOLAS HAYEK IS ONE of the oldest working businessmen in Switzerland. He can look back over a 60-year career. So it is not surprising that Hayek has a deeply ambiguous relationship with the subject of time. 'I hate time because it cannot be grasped or stopped. But I also love it because it has given me so much', he said one year before his 80th birthday on Radio DRS. Hayek owes a fulfilled life to time. But not only that: over the years he has earnt billions in assets. Hayek likes to compare himself with Scrooge McDuck. He has given himself this nickname in many interviews. Walt Disney's comic figure swimming in money is his role-model.

Like this richest duck in the world, Hayek is also extremely thrifty. Although he went from being a multimillionaire to a multibillionaire in just a few years, he has not changed his lifestyle. Hayek still lives by Lake Hallwil in Meisterschwanden. His house is certainly fine and large, but it is far from ostentatious. He does not have a private lake landing stage, as is common at many executives' villas on the Zurich gold coast. His wife Marianne spends her time not at a smart golf club but tending her garden. Hayek has owned the holiday villa called Castel du Cap, with a tennis court and swimming pool, in Cap d'Antibes in southern France ever since he was a business consultant.

Hayek's capital has been reduced by several billion francs, though, by the stock market crash triggered in 2008. This halved the Swatch share price within a year. That does not seem to concern Hayek particularly. He is much more annoyed in a very general way by the devastating repercussions of the financial crisis on the productive real economy. 'I am often asked if I am worried – and I am not. But I am furious', he said in the magazine section of the German weekly newspaper *Die Zeit*. When the major bank UBS had to report one write-down after another, Hayek fulminated on western Swiss television with a shaking voice against the speculators 'with no moral conscience' who had triggered this crisis. In one of his interviews he even used the term 'financial bandits'.

For Hayek, the loss in value of his stakeholding is relative, for this is only a paper loss. It would be a real reduction in value if he wanted to sell his stake. But that was never his intention. The watch magnate is firmly convinced that his company is worth much more than is stated in the stock exchange prices. The short-termist investors, though, have so far hardly been infected by Hayek's optimism. The mood among stock exchange speculators and the recommendations of the bank analysts is what actually determines the market prices. This powerlessness against the financial markets has always intensely annoyed Hayek as a man of action. He does not consider the 'acrobats and jugglers in the financial circus' to be capable of correctly assessing long-term industrial strategies. Amid all the criticism, Hayek also has some cause to be grateful to the analysts. Even when he took over the watch company, the doom-mongers were talking down the share price and so enabled him to acquire his shareholding at an extremely low price. Most investors then believed neither in the company nor in the group of investors led by Hayek. It is this unpredictability of the financial markets and its operators that irritates Hayek. Uncertain consumers who take a pessimistic view of their financial future are in no mood to go and buy a new watch, and if bankers' bonuses are either reduced or cancelled, this has a direct impact on the sales of expensive watches.

In the long-term, however, the Swatch Group is in an extremely good position. The slogan 'time is money' assumes a totally different meaning with Hayek. Over the years, he has built up a huge empire by satisfying a basic human need to measure time. The once penniless Lebanese immigrant now reigns over the biggest watch company in the world, with 19 brands and around 160 factories. The brand value of Omega, Swatch and Breguet alone is estimated to be around 4 billion francs by the consultancy firm Interbrand, Zintzmeyer & Lux. The stock market capitalisation, the market value of the Swatch Group security, has risen within around 20 years from 1 billion francs to many times that amount. Depending on the stock market sentiment, this sum is now in the region of 10–20 billion francs.

Hayek has put most of the profits generated into developing the company. Over the years he has invested around 10 billion francs in production and distribution. Unlike many other companies, he has not done this with bank loans. His company is debt-free. The Swatch Group is solvent enough to be able to repay all its liabilities in one go at any time. The real estate has been completely amortised for years. The share of its own means in the balance sheet total stood as high as 75 per cent in 2008. Only a few Swiss firms are so solidly financed. On financial matters Hayek is a very conservative-minded entrepreneur. He has achieved great independence with this formula. This pays off especially well in crisis periods when banks are reluctant to lend.

Hayek has achieved the phenomenal expansion of his watch company in the past two decades almost exclusively through internal growth. Certainly, over the years he has bought another series of firms. Yet these companies were never as large or as profitable at the time of the acquisition as they have been since under the auspices of the Swatch Group. Hayek created thousands of new jobs. He doubled the number of employees to over 24,000 staff. The vast majority of them work in Switzerland. Today, every third employee working in the Swiss watch industry is employed by the Swatch Group. Hayek has also created work for many suppliers with his contracts.

Anyone who wants to know where Hayek earns so much money has to fumble in the dark, though. The company only gives out benchmark financial data. Detailed results from the individual product groups and brands are not published. Bank analysts, financial journalists and investors have to make do with estimates here. The watch boss claims that he does not freely want to give his rivals a competitive advantage by letting them look into his books. Rolex, for example, Omega's strongest competitor, is actually much more secretive. Rolex, though, is not listed on the stock exchange. As a purely private enterprise, the company is not publicly accountable.

It is not only the Swatch Group's reticent information policy that is criticised by investors. Deficiencies in control and supervision are also criticised. So the Ethos Foundation has long been complaining that the board of directors is too dependent on Hayek as the major investor and that it is superannuated. The Ethos head, Dominique Biedermann, has repeatedly called for the board of directors to be elected individually rather than in corpore. He has so far been fighting a losing battle with this demand, for the general meetings held early every year at the conference centre in Biel are always a home match for Hayek. To date, the patriarch has always been easily able to shoot down suggestions made by shareholders. All votes are taken by a show of hands, which otherwise is only customary in pure family businesses.

To Hayek, shareholder stability is a major issue. He believes he can only safeguard this continuity by keeping everything under his own control. The kind of turbulence that has been experienced in the past by highly traditional Swiss companies such as Sulzer, Saurer, Unaxis or Valora through attacks from corporate raiders fills him with horror. Certainly it was known a few years ago that in addition to Hayek himself, the American Capital Group and the throat-pastille heiress Esther Grether, there was also a third important investor with a stakeholding of around 4 per cent in the company. Yet the fear that the Swatch Group might become a football of speculatively minded investors is unfounded. Hayek has a firm grip on his empire. He runs it almost like a family-owned SME. As president and delegate, the senior boss still largely sets the tone today, both on the board of directors and in the group management, as well as with the brand managers and regional managers; that is, at all three levels of the hierarchy.

Hayek can easily afford to dismiss the arguments and criticisms made by the small shareholders. He does not need the small investors. He has enough money in his coffers to finance the further development of the company. Unlike many other stock exchange-listed firms, he therefore has never buttered up bank analysts and fund managers at road-shows in order to entice new investors. He also does not try to attract investors with a generous dividend policy.

Instead of attracting attention with a generous payout policy, Hayek prefers to invest the profits in expanding the distribution. As a clever calculator, he does not want to leave the margin to the trade but channel the increased revenue in the value chain into the funds of the Swatch Group. Hayek is still lagging behind his competitors, especially Richemont, in this respect. Admittedly, there are already around 50 Omega flagship stores and around 100 Swatch stores today. However, Cartier alone has around 250 sales outlets of its own. But Hayek wants to catch up. While other firms are radically slashing their budgets in the crisis, Hayek is working against the trend: he wants to open a dozen new Omega flagship stores in China, as well as one in New York and a Tourbillon boutique on Wall Street. Furthermore, in Shanghai for the world exhibition in 2010 at the legendary Peace Hotel on the Bund, a form of art centre with luxury watches is being built at a cost of $30 million. In China, Hayek is especially well placed in relation to the competition, with an estimated turnover share of around 20 per cent.

Hayek is paying most attention today to the prestige brands Omega, Breguet and Blancpain. These have now taken over from the Swatch as the moneyspinners of the group. Hayek also applies his mass production philosophy to the high-end brands. According to the Zurich Kantonalbank's estimate, two thirds of the finished watches turnover already fall into the high price segment. The luxury brands have enormous potential. Since Hayek took over Breguet, the turnover has multiplied tenfold. And at Blancpain, around 10,000 watches are now being produced every year. Even at Longines and Tissot, the longer-established brands, a price upgrade is under way.

The Swatch, however, established in the lower price segment, is no longer the bestseller that it used to be. Certainly, since it was launched, around 400 million of these watches have been sold. But the days when customers still had to queue to get hold of one of these fashion watches are long gone. The Swatch has become an ordinary consumer item. Whereas in the record year of 1993 around 26 million Swatches were sold, in the last few years it has not even been half that number. So the economies of scale are gradually diminishing. In other words, the smaller the quantities produced, the fewer the possible savings on unit costs. The Swatch is certainly still a market leader in the mass market. It still provides around half the Swiss watch exports in unit terms. But the erosion process cannot be overlooked. Experts in the industry point out that there are too many models on the market and that the watch is no longer instantly recognisable for the consumer as the Swatch. A study by the advertising agency Advico Young and Rubicam showed that the Swatch has lost its image to the younger generation. In 1995 it was still the number one in this ranking. 'The brand has lost its earlier rebellious appearance; what used to be a cult brand is today only mediocrity', according to Caspar Coppetti, the author of the study. This does not have to be the case. The decline of a brand is not inevitable. The timeless success of Coca Cola, Rolex or in fact even Omega clearly demonstrates that.

Certainly, Swatch still tries from time to time to attract attention with unconventional methods; for example, a few years ago in the USA with the Bunnysutra model. For weeks a Swatch with two rabbits trying out Kama Sutra positions hung in Times Square in New York.

Some people found it amusing, while Christian fundamentalists saw it as a threat to sexual morality. But the marketing people had achieved their objective: the Swatch was being talked about again on almost all the American TV stations. Yet such targeted stunts have no long-term impact. Even the internet advertising clips on YouTube lack the wit and originality of the pioneering days.

There is still a great dormant potential in the cheap watches sector. China today already produces over one billion. More than six billion consumers worldwide qualify as buyers of 'normal' watches costing under 100 francs. But according to *Forbes* magazine, there are only still around 800 billionaires worldwide, around one third fewer than before the financial crisis. Only these super-rich can afford expensive watches costing millions of francs. The flight to the pinnacle of the price pyramid entails the hidden danger of a resulting erosion of the industrial base. In the watch industry at present, a dangerous development is currently emerging against which Hayek had always previously warned. The average price of Swiss watches has constantly risen in the last few years. At the same time, the number of units produced is falling. This trend can also be observed at the Swatch Group.

Ernst Thomke, Hayek's former right-hand man, calls this shift towards the upper price segment the 'Rolls Royce effect': even this luxury brand could not exist in the market all on its own. The former British national treasure could only survive through technological collaboration with VW and BMW. So the longer-term prospects for Omega are partly dependent on the success of the Swatch. Hayek seems to be aware of the danger. 'We are at risk of experiencing exactly the same problem as 25 years ago', he warned early in 2008 in the *Tribune de Genève*. Certainly, this comment was directed much less at his own company than at the whole industry, for unlike the Swatch Group, most watch firms ignore the mass market of cheap watches. To Hayek's annoyance, they are also not particularly concerned about the movements and parts production that is strategically important for the Swiss watch industry.

Hayek regards this as a further dangerous development. Apart from Rolex, almost all the manufacturers are in fact dependent on the supply by the Swatch Group. The Swiss watch firms have hardly developed any initiative of their own in this domain. In practically all Swiss watches, the regulating parts (balance springs) come from

Hayek's company Nivarox. His company also supplies almost the whole watch industry with raw movements. The technological skill is thus still largely concentrated in the Swatch Group. This guarantees the technological independence of the Swiss watch industry. Despite its high efficiency, the parts productions only contributes a small proportion of the company profit.

Hayek has repeatedly had to endure criticism for this strong market position in the last few years. He has never striven for this dominance. It is rather a legacy of the pre-Second World War period when the State had ordered the concentration of the raw movements production at ASUAG. The watch industry got used to this historically developed division of labour. It was also extremely comfortable for most firms. They could always count on being stocked by the Swatch Group. So a cry of horror went up through the industry a few years ago when Hayek announced that ETA would cease to supply third-party firms with raw movements from 2005. Some manufacturers claimed that the watch magnate was seeking to bankrupt his competitors by stopping these supplies. The competition commission (Weko) was called in. It investigated whether there was an abuse of market power according to the relevant anti-cartel law. The competition watchdogs then struck a good Swiss compromise: the Swatch Group's customers were given a period up to 2011 to get their own raw movement production going. From this point, Hayek is free to stop supplies to third parties. Instead of the economically conditioned ebb and flow of orders coming in, he will then be able to adapt the production entirely to the needs of his own brands. Yet at the end of 2008, several watch manufacturers lodged a further complaint with the competition commission – this time because ETA was raising its prices for raw movements. Hayek was again criticised for an abuse of market power.

Certainly, Hayek almost makes the weather today in the industry. But this strong market position is the result of his visionary strategy consistently pursued over the years, and therefore of his success. Success can inspire envy. In the competition and among the specialist dealers, Hayek therefore does not have only friends. Even some famous watch shops criticise him for dictating the terms of their supplies. Yet his critics are almost exclusively in the watch industry. Among the Swiss public, Hayek has acquired high regard through his services to Switzerland as a manufacturing base. As a businessman, he makes a pleasant change from all the 'helicopter managers' who land, throw up dust, and fly back again with their pockets full. Hayek was one of the few Swiss business leaders who very early recognised the importance of this manufacturing base and the dangers of an excessively powerful financial sector. The difficulties that beset Switzerland with the UBS cluster risk have proved him right.

Since the severe financial crisis exposed the incompetence of some arrogant managers, credible, down-to-earth entrepreneurs have been increasingly in demand among citizens. Hayek today is the supreme model entrepreneur. In popularity, his company is in second place among 125 Swiss firms after the air rescue service, as a survey by the market research institute IHA-GfK has shown. Only Hayek has been showered in his lifetime with so many honours from home and abroad. Even the town of Biel, which he has often harshly criticised, has made him an honorary citizen.

So Hayek has already become a legend in his own lifetime. This favour was not even granted to such outstanding pioneers as the railway chief Alfred Escher or the Migros founder Gottlieb Duttweiler. They were unlucky that their contributions were only truly understood and honoured by posterity. Hayek may absolutely be named in the same breath as these business figures. He is not only the 'saviour of the Swiss watch industry'. He has made his mark on the entire Swiss economy.

Index

Compiled by Sue Carlton

Page numbers in **bold** refer to photographs

NGH refers to Nicolas Georges Hayek